Foundations of Modern Sociology Series

Alex Inkeles, *Editor*

Foundations of Modern Sociology Series

the sociology of religion

Thomas F. O'Dea, *Columbia University*

Prentice-Hall, Inc., *Englewood Cliffs, New Jersey*

Prentice-Hall Foundations of Modern Sociology Series

Alex Inkeles, *Editor*

Current printing (last digit):

11   10   9   8   7

PRENTICE-HALL INTERNATIONAL, INC., *London*
PRENTICE-HALL OF AUSTRALIA, PTY., LTD., *Sydney*
PRENTICE-HALL OF CANADA, LTD., *Toronto*
PRENTICE-HALL OF INDIA PRIVATE LIMITED, *New Delhi*
PRENTICE-HALL OF JAPAN, INC., *Tokyo*

C–82138(p), C–82139(c)

/

preface

This small book is offered as an introduction to the sociology of religion. It is, however, more than that. It is also a book about "theory," taking that word in the scientific sense to mean a body of ideas and concepts which delineate a realm of study in terms of both research problems and generalized conclusions. Such a conceptual scheme and vocabulary of analysis is presented here. It is presented concretely, eschewing high level generalizations without immediate empirical reference, and using as little technical jargon as possible. Theory is here presented in the form of empirical material, conceptualized as problems and empirical generalizations based on research, rather than as abstract formulations.

As scientific theory, providing a frame of reference for thinking and research, the conceptual arsenal of the sociology of religion is quite impressive. It represents the contributions of numerous scholars over several generations, from Vico and Comte to contemporary workers in the field. The contributions of some of these figures, such as Durkheim and Weber, are especially significant. But it is a group product to which many sociologists and other scholars have contributed significantly. As a frame of reference defining problems and as a set of empirical generalizations derived from past studies, it is, however, incomplete, and in need of considerably increased precise formulation. Both its strengths and its weaknesses in these respects will be evident to the readers of this book. In a technical sense, the sociology of religion is but one aspect of the study of the relationship between ideas and ideals embodied in movements and institutions, and the social situations of their origin, development, flourishing, and decline. The significant analogies between religion and such secularized religious surrogates as nationalism and socialism are also indicated in this work.

While presenting an introduction to the sociology of religion and a statement of the body of theory existing in the field, this book also gives the lay reader a brief presentation of the sociological approach to an interpretation of religious phenomena, and thereby offers him one important avenue for understanding the human significance of religion.

The author wishes to express his thanks to all those who have helped him in the preparation of this book, to all those scholars upon whose insights he has drawn, to the staff of Prentice-Hall, to the editor of this Foundations series, Alex Inkeles, who read and criticized earlier drafts of these chapters, and to David Brewer and Ellen Besse, who aided with the reading and correction of the final version. Thanks are also expressed to the numerous publishers who gave permission to use the quotations in the text and who are acknowledged in the footnotes.

Thomas F. O'Dea

contents

vii

contents

religion and society: the functionalist approach

one

No explanation of religion can be complete without considering its sociological aspects. Religion, concerned as it is with shared beliefs and practices, is pre-eminently social, and until modern times was to be found universally in every human society of which we have any record, including those whose remains have been uncovered and interpreted by archaeologists. Yet the question immediately arises how this ubiquitous and significant kind of social behavior is to be understood; how indeed it is to be approached from the sociological point of view.

In established societies, religion is one of the important institutional structures making up the total social system. Yet religion is unlike government and law, which are concerned with the allocation and restraint of power. It is unlike economic institutions, which are concerned with work, production and exchange. And it is unlike the institution of the family, which regulates and patterns the relationships between the sexes, between generations, and among those related by consanguinity and affinity. The central interest of religion appears to concern something comparatively vague and intangible, whose empirical reality is far from clear. It is concerned with a "beyond," with man's relation to and attitude toward that "beyond," and with what men consider to be the practical implications of the "beyond" for human life. It is concerned with something that, to use the phrase of the

Italian sociologist Vilfredo Pareto, "transcends experience," taking experience to mean, as it did for Pareto, the observable events of our everyday existence, or their refined and systematic treatment in science.

A comparison of religion with other human activities, or of religious institutions with other social institutions, might suggest that religion, with its reference to an intangible beyond, is something unimportant and evanescent, something peripheral to the genuine business of human life. Yet the facts point to something else. Indeed, religious institutions are generally held to have a special importance, to be concerned with an aspect of the human situation that, precisely in its transcendence of the commonplace, involves something of pre-eminent significance for men. Moreover, history reveals that religious institutions have been the most viable forms of human association.

Religion has been characterized as embodying the most sublime of human aspirations; as being a bulwark of morality, a source of public order and inner individual peace; as ennobling and civilizing in its effect upon mankind. It has also been accused of being a stubborn obstacle retarding progress, and of promoting fanaticism and intolerance, ignorance, superstition, and obscurantism. The record reveals religion to be among the strongest buttresses of an established social order. It also, however, shows it capable of exhibiting profound revolutionary tendencies, as in the Peasant War in sixteenth-century Germany. Emile Durkheim, the pioneer French sociologist of religion, proposed that religion was the source of all higher culture; Marx declared that it was the opium of the people. That it represents a set of human activities and a complex of social forms of considerable significance cannot be denied. The question arises, however: How is the sociologist to approach most effectively the observation and analysis of this many-sided and ambiguous aspect of man's social existence?

Functional Theory

Much that is worthwhile in the growing research into the sociology of religion has been significantly influenced by a sociological point of view called "functional theory." As a frame of reference for empirical research, functional theory sees society as an ongoing equilibrium of social institutions which pattern human activity in terms of shared norms, held to be legitimate and binding by the human participants themselves. This complex of institutions, which as a whole constitutes the *social system,* is such that each part (each institutional element) is interdependent with all the other parts, and that changes in any part affect the others, and the condition of the system as a whole. In these terms, religion is but one form of institutionalized human behavior. Hence the question arises: What is the contribution of each institutional complex to the maintenance of the social system? Such contributions may be either obvious or subtle. They may be such that the human actors understand them, but they may also be beyond the actors' awareness. That is to say, a social institution has both *manifest* and *latent* functions as

2

part of a total social system.[1] With respect to our subject the question arises: What are the functions, manifest and latent, of religious institutions in maintaining the equilibrium of the social system as a whole? Moreover, functional theory views culture as a more or less integrated body of knowledge, pseudo-knowledge, beliefs, and values. These define the human situation and the conditions of action for the members of a society. Culture, understood in this way, is a symbolic system of meanings, some of which define reality as it is believed to be, others of which define normative expectations incumbent on humans. The elements making up the system of cultural meanings may be either implicit or explicit. A cultural system of meanings displays some degree of meaningful integration and strain toward consistency. Culture is integrated with the social system in that it enters into the definitions of means and ends, of proscriptions and prescriptions, of the permitted and the forbidden, by defining the roles within which a society's members confront the established expectations of their social situation. Religion, with its transcendent reference to a beyond, is an important aspect of this cultural phenomenon. *Culture is the creation by man of a world of adjustment and meaning, in the context of which human life can be significantly lived.* Thus culture enters deeply into the thinking and feeling of men and is central to the social forms which emerge from their actions. In the words of the pioneer American student of religion, Wendell T. Bush, ". . . religion is a very important part of the world of imagination that functions socially, and its verbal expressions represent only a small fraction of it." [2] The question arises analogous to our first: What is the contribution of religion to culture as a system?

Contemporary sociologists recognize that although men share values, ideas, and patterned orientations which affect their behavior; although they act in institutionalized contexts, in situations in which role expectations, enforced by positive and negative sanctions, pattern their actual performance —nevertheless, it is the individual human being who acts, and thinks, and feels. Sociology today has outgrown and discarded earlier theories which, groping for an explanation of the patterning and sharing characteristic of human activity, postulated ideas of a "group mind" and other, similar, confused formulations. It also recognizes the contributions of personality psychology, and has taken for its point of reference in this regard the human personality, a somewhat systematic complex of drives, needs, propensities to respond and act, values, and so on. It recognizes the personality as a system patterned by learning and with an autonomy of its own. Personality systems, of course, are not "situationless egos" (or even "situationless" combinations of egos, ids, and superegos), but rather exist within socially structured situations. Moreover, a significant part of personality systems is the result of

[1] Robert K. Merton, *Social Theory and Social Structure* (Glencoe, Ill.: The Free Press, 1958), Chap. 1, "Manifest and Latent Functions: Toward the Codification of Functional Analysis in Sociology," pp. 19–84.

[2] Quoted from Horace L. Friess, "Growth of Study of Religion at Columbia University, 1924–1954," *The Review of Religion* (November 1954), Nos. 1 and 2, 19:15.

learning—the internalization of important aspects of the culture. Hence, it becomes necessary to ask the functional question again, this time in the context of a functional theory of personality: What is the function of religion with respect to the ongoing equilibrium of personality?

Since culture, social system, and personality are three aspects of a complex, integrated social phenomenon whose effects we observe in human behavior, any one of the three functional questions we have asked implies the other two. In answering any one of the three functional questions we have formulated, we must of necessity answer it in terms of the other two as well.

Functional theory sees man in society as characterized by two types of needs and two kinds of propensities to act. Men must act upon the environment, either adjusting to it or mastering and controlling it, to insure their own survival. A human society with its culture is the unit of human survival and societies often require the death of some of their members to insure their own survival. The history of humanity reveals that men have progressively increased their capacity to control their environment and influence the conditions of their lives. But men are not simply makers of things and manipulators of environmental conditions. Human activity is not simply adaptive and manipulative. Men also express feelings, act out felt needs, respond to persons and things in non-utilitarian ways, and enter into relationships. As the American sociologist George C. Homans has put it, men never confine themselves to those "activities, interactions and sentiments" necessary for the survival of the group, but elaborate these elements far beyond survival requirements.[3] Men also have expressive needs, and in their very problem-solving tasks work out relationships among themselves and with their situation.[4] Indeed, modern psychology has revealed, over and above what may become obvious in a common-sense reading of human history, the tremendous importance—in fact, the crucial character—of such expressive needs.

What is the significance of religion in terms of these adaptive and expressive needs of human beings? Since these needs find their outlet and expression in terms of culture patterns within the context of social systems, an answer to our first three functional questions must include an answer to this one as well. It is an axiom of functional theory that what has no function ceases to exist. Since religion has continued to exist from time immemorial it obviously must have a function, or even a complex of functions.

Functional theory sees the contribution of religion to human societies and cultures to be based upon its central characteristic: its transcendence of everyday experience in the natural environment. Why should men need "something that transcends experience," or, to use Talcott Parsons' term, a "transcendental reference," something "beyond" the empirical? Why should societies need such beliefs and practices and the institutions which embody

[3] George C. Homans, *The Human Group* (New York: Harcourt, Brace & World, Inc., 1950), p. 108.

[4] Robert F. Bales, *Interaction Process Analysis* (Cambridge, Mass.: Addison-Wesley, 1950), Chap. 2.

4

religion and society: the functionalist approach

and preserve them? Functional theory sees such need as the result of three fundamental characteristics of human existence. First, man lives in conditions of uncertainty; events of crucial significance to his safety and welfare are beyond his prevision. Human existence, in other words, is characterized by *contingency*. Second, man's capacity to control and affect the conditions of his life, although increasing, is inherently limited. At a certain point, man's condition with respect to the conflict between his wants and his environment is characterized by *powerlessness*. Third, men must live in a society, and a society is an orderly allocation of functions, facilities, and rewards. It involves both a division of labor and a division of product. It requires imperative coordination—that is, some degree of superordination and subordination in the relations of men. Moreover, societies exist amid conditions of *scarcity*— the third fundamental characteristic of human existence. The requirements of order in scarcity cause differential distribution of goods and values, and thus relative deprivation. Thus functional theory sees the role of religion as assisting men to adjust to the three brute facts of *contingency, powerlessness,* and *scarcity* (and, consequently, *frustration* and *deprivation*). These are existential characteristics of the human condition in terms of functional theory, and are therefore inherent to some degree in all human societies. Religion in these terms is seen as the most basic "mechanism" of adjustment to the aleatory and frustrating elements.

Contingency, or the "uncertainty context," refers to the fact that all human ventures, no matter how carefully planned or expertly executed, are liable to disappointment. And since such ventures are often characterized by a high degree of emotional involvement, such disappointment brings with it deep human injury. Even in our advanced technological society, fortune remains a capricious and uncertain goddess, and it is still true that "the best laid plans of mice and men gang aft agley."

Powerlessness, or the "impossibility context," refers to the fact that not everything men desire can be attained. Death, suffering, coercion—these characterize our existence. The evils we suffer from those vulnerabilities to which our flesh is heir and those which we inflict upon one another wittingly and unwittingly mar our existence and deprive us of satisfactions and happiness.

Human contingency and powerlessness, man's experience in the uncertainty and impossibility contexts, carry human beings beyond the established and defined situations of everyday social behavior and everyday cultural definitions of goals and norms. As inherent characteristics of the human condition, contingency and powerlessness bring men face-to-face with situations in which established techniques and mundane social prescriptions display a total insufficiency for providing "mechanisms" for adjustment. They confront men with "breaking points" in the socially structured round of daily behavior. As "breaking beyond" ordinary experience, they raise questions which can find an answer only in some kind of "beyond" itself.

At these "breaking points," what Max Weber has called "the problem of meaning" arises in the severest and most poignant manner. Why should I die? Why should a loved one die, and in unfulfilled youth? Why did that venture, in which our heart's desire reposed, go awry? Why illness? Such

5

questions demand meaningful answers. If they are found to be without meaning, the value of institutionalized goals and norms is undermined. How can morale be maintained when disappointment lurks at every step, and death, the ultimate disappointment, strikes at our utter defenselessness in the end?

To the evils which beset men in terms of the contingency and powerlessness of their natural condition must be added the frustrations and deprivations inherent in human society.[5] The allocations of function, facility, and reward which constitute the basic structure of society are made differentially and under conditions of scarcity. There are *haves* and *have nots*. Moreover, order implies authority, and authority requires subordination. Control and supervision often prove as frustrating as deprivation. The question arises: Why obey rules and laws, why abide by norms, why meet socially accepted expectations, when they impose hardships upon us? And even worse, when they impose hardships upon us while others apparently thrive. Society and culture say that what is required, advised, prescribed, will be rewarded, both in terms of material and non-material rewards. But too often "the good die young and the evil flourish as the green bay tree." The problem of meaning arises as to the "Why?" of this unhappy aspect of our human condition. And unless this "Why?" is answered, our morale founders and our acceptance of norms and goals (which normally often inflict frustration upon us anyway) is undermined. Obviously, ongoing human activity and the continued functioning of the social system require some answer to the problem of meaning. If a "larger view" which transcends empirical experience in the here-and-now in which we encounter these evils can be formulated, if norms and goals which work hardship upon us appear justified in such a view, then misfortune and frustration will make some ultimate sense. Then life can be viewed as having meaning, a meaning supplied by a view of it which transcends empirical experience in the finite human situation of the here-and-now. The here-and-now becomes meaningful by being fitted into a beyond.

Functional theory focuses our attention on the functional contribution of religion to the social system. Religion, by its reference to a beyond and its beliefs concerning man's relationship to that beyond, provides a supraempirical view of a larger total reality. In the context of this reality, the disappointments and frustrations inflicted on mankind by uncertainty and impossibility, and by the institutionalized order of human society, may be seen as meaningful in some ultimate sense, and this makes acceptance of and adjustment to them possible. Moreover, by showing the norms and rules of society to be part of a larger supraempirical ethical order, ordained and sanctified by religious belief and practice, religion contributes to their enforcement when adherence to them contradicts the wishes or interests of those affected. Religion answers the problem of meaning. It sanctifies the norms of the established social order at what we have called the "breaking points," by providing a grounding for the beliefs and orientations of men in a view of

---

[5] In some ways the best treatment of this problem is still Sigmund Freud, *Civilization and Its Discontents*, ed. and trans. by James Strachey (New York: Norton, 1961).

religion and society: the functionalist approach

reality that transcends the empirical here-and-now of daily experience. Moreover, men not only require answers to the problem of meaning in terms of their cognitive orientation to their world, they also, as we have noted above, act out needs and enter into relationships. It is a salient aspect of most religions that they offer ritual and liturgy, enabling men to enter into relationships with God, gods, or other sacred forces, and to act out responses and feelings involved in those relationships. Thus not only is cognitive frustration overcome, which is involved in the problem of meaning, but the emotional adjustments to frustrations and deprivations inherent in human life and human society are facilitated.

Functional theory in this way provides answers to the four questions which it raises and through which it provides access to an understanding of the social significance of religious phenomena. It also provides the possibility of understanding another nearly universal phenomenon, one intimately related to religion itself: magic. Magic as a set of beliefs and practices is, in one form or another, characteristic of human societies. It shares with religion the conception of a beyond—the idea of supraempirical aspects of reality. It also shares with religion the idea that men are capable of establishing some kind of contact with such supraempirical realities. However, whereas religious ritual claims only to place men in relation to such forces and realities and expresses the human response to them, magical ritual claims to offer ways of manipulating these forces to bring about changes and effect consequences in the empirical world itself. Yet, like religion, magic also offers ways of adjusting to those aspects of the human situation which admittedly lie beyond the control or influence of human effort, guided though it may be by rational and empirical techniques of adaptation or mastery.

Religion has been defined in terms of functional theory as *the manipulation of non-empirical or supraempirical means for non-empirical or supraempirical ends;* magic as *the manipulation of non-empirical or supraempirical means for empirical ends.* But the use of the term "manipulation" in the definition of religion is inaccurate and fails to describe adequately the religious attitude. Religion offers what is felt to be a way of entering into a relationship with the supraempirical aspects of reality, be they conceived as God, gods, or otherwise. Magic differs from religion in that it is manipulative in essence; yet magical manipulation too is conducted in an atmosphere of fear and respect, marvel and wonder, similar to that which characterizes the religious relationship.

The Functions of Religion and Magic

What we have been saying here can be illustrated by the treatment of religion and magic in the study of the Trobriand Islanders by Bronislaw Malinowski. Malinowski noted that the inhabitants of these islands possess considerable empirical knowledge and skill with respect to fishing and gardening, their means of subsistence. They regard magic as indispensable to the success of gardening. Although no one knew what would happen without the use of magic, since no one had neglected to make use

7

of it when Malinowski made his study, nevertheless without it, it was believed that certain disaster would befall men's efforts. Yet the Trobriander did not attribute all his success to magic. He was aware of natural causes and conditions and of his own mental and physical effort to control them. "If fences are broken down, if the seed is destroyed or has been dried or washed away, he will have recourse not to magic but to work, guided by knowledge and reason." But he also knows that despite all his knowledge and effort, success may not follow. Results are affected by forces and agencies outside his sphere of control; the good harvest, like the poor one, is the result of unknown and uncontrollable elements. Failure may well be the result of "ill luck and bad chance" despite "all his most strenuous efforts and best-founded knowledge. To control these influences and these only he employs magic."

Malinowski emphasizes the consciousness of this distinction in the thinking of the Trobrianders—the distinction between empirical elements of everyday experience and the forces and agencies of a supraempirical character that lie beyond human control. He refers to this distinction as a "clear-cut division" in the Islander's mind, respecting the condition affecting gardening. The empirical conditions subject to control "are coped with by knowledge and work," the supraempirical conditions, "by magic." [6]

It follows from Malinowski's analysis that recourse to magic should become more important as the reliability of empirical knowledge and practical skills diminishes. He sees fishing in the Islands as a crucial test. In villages on the inner lagoon, fish are poisoned. It is an easy method and yields abundant results. It also requires no risks and involves no dangers. Trobrianders also fish in the open sea. Here the method is far less reliable, and danger is involved. Malinowski notes that the Islanders use no magic in connection with safe and reliable lagoon fishing, but that in deep-sea fishing, with its uncertainty and danger, "there is extensive magical ritual to secure safety and good results." [7]

Malinowski distinguishes between religion and magic by pointing out that magic has an end, in pursuit of which the magical ritual is performed. He contrasts the magical rite performed to prevent death in childbirth, and the religious rite which celebrates the birth of the child. The first "has a definite practical purpose which is known to all who practice it and can be easily elicited from any native informant." The religious rite, ". . . say a presentation of a new-born or a feast of rejoicing in the event, has no purpose: it is not a means to an end but an end in itself." The religious rite "expresses the feelings" of all concerned. "While in the magical act the underlying idea and aim is always clear, straightforward and definite, in the religious ceremony there is no purpose directed toward a subsequent event." [8]

For Malinowski, magic and religion are similar in that they both "arise and function in situations of emotional stress," both "open up escapes from such situations and such impasses as offer no empirical way out except by

[6] Bronislaw Malinowski, *Magic, Science and Religion* (Glencoe, Ill.: The Free Press, 1954), pp. 28–29.
[7] *Ibid.*, pp. 30–31.
[8] *Ibid.*, pp. 37–38.

8

ritual and belief into the domain of the supernatural," both are "based strictly on mythological tradition," both "exist in the atmosphere of the miraculous," and both are "surrounded by taboos and observances which mark off their acts from those of the profane world." But religion and magic differ in that magic aims at a practical end while religion is "a body of self-contained acts being themselves the fulfillment of their purpose." Moreover, magical beliefs are simple, while religion offers a more complex and more varied supernatural sphere. Magic "has its limited, circumscribed technique: spell, rite, and the condition of the performer form always its trite trinity." Religion, in contrast, has "complex aspects and purposes"; it is "more varied" and "more creative." [9]

Magic supplements man's practical abilities and thereby enhances his confidence. Its function "is to ritualize man's optimism, to enhance his faith in the victory of hope over fear." Religion, on the other hand, contributes to man's morale by enhancing "all valuable mental attitudes, such as reverence for tradition, harmony with environment, courage and confidence in the struggle with difficulty and at the prospect of death." Religious belief ". . . embodied and maintained by cult and ceremonial, has an immense biological value, and so reveals to primitive man truth in the wider, pragmatic sense of the word." [10] Thus religion is seen as human response. It is engendered in situations which involve frustration and deprivation arising from contingency, powerlessness, and scarcity. It is embodied in social forms that enable men to confront and adjust to misfortune. It is "the sole means of adjustment to the dark mystery which in all ages surrounds the slight circle of human knowledge." [11] In the words of George Santayana:

> Our knowledge is a torch of smoky pine
> That lights the pathway but one step ahead
> Across a void of mystery and dread.

Religion provides definition beyond the extent of our knowledge, and security beyond the guarantees of human relationships.

Commenting on Malinowski's analysis, a fellow anthropologist, A. R. Radcliffe-Brown, has suggested an alternative hypothesis which raises another side of the issue for us. He contends that for certain rites one could as easily maintain a contrary theory, ". . . that if it were not for the existence of the rite and the beliefs associated with it the individual would feel no anxiety, and that the psychological effect of the rite is to create in him a sense of insecurity or danger." [12] He suggests that the Andaman Islander, whose society he had studied, would not observe food taboos if it were not for the rituals and beliefs which ostensibly protect him from danger but actually

[9] *Ibid.,* pp. 87–88.
[10] *Ibid.,* pp. 89–90.
[11] William Graham Sumner and Albert Galloway Keller, *The Science of Society,* Vol. II (New Haven: Yale University Press, 1927), p. 1466.
[12] A. R. Radcliffe-Brown, *Taboo* (Cambridge: Cambridge University Press, 1938), p. 39.

9

arouse his anxiety. It is Radcliffe-Brown's contention that magic and rite arouse, as well as allay, anxiety.

George C. Homans, in a suggestive reconciliation of these differences, has pointed out that "Rightly understood, he [Malinowski] does not say that the natives feel anxiety in dangerous situations but that they would do so if the rites of magic were not performed. And the facts that Radcliffe-Brown cites, instead of supporting a theory opposed to Malinowski, follow directly from it." [13] In fact, Malinowski points out that, in situations of danger, human reactions *engender* rites. Once established and institutionalized, such rites first arouse the sense of danger, and then alleviate it.

The contrast in the views of Malinowski and Radcliffe-Brown focuses our attention on the difference between two quite different situations. Malinowski is concerned with two things: the situations in which rites originate, and the function they perform once they are established. Radcliffe-Brown does not concern himself with the situations in which rites are engendered. He concentrates his attention on how they function—that is, on their arousing and allaying of anxiety, once they are established. The disagreement between the two eminent anthropologists calls our attention to the important fact that rites are not spontaneous reactions to dangerous situations, but rather are institutionalized performances. They derive from what originally were spontaneous responses, which have become elaborated and standardized. Once established, they reinstate in a formal way the conditions of their origin. In doing this, they both arouse and allay anxiety, as Radcliffe-Brown has made clear, but they also perform the function attributed to them by Malinowski. They protect the individual against contingency and danger by anticipating them and coping with them symbolically. In this way they allay the anxiety which the situation would create for people without the pattern response, and avoid the disorganizing effects it would have had.

Rites in both religion and magic display two characteristics: (1) reinstatement of an earlier situation, with the arousal and catharsis of appropriate feelings; and (2) the displacement of attention from some aspects of the situation and the focusing of it upon others. (The distinction between situations of origin and situations in which institutionalized behavior is involved is a significant one to which we shall return in Chapter 2.) Thus both the magical and religious rite anticipate and arouse the anxieties they allay. Moreover, both concentrate attention on some aspects of the situation and deflect attention away from others, often those which it would be difficult to handle even symbolically. Here an important question arises: To what extent do institutionalized religion and magic represent a net gain for men, with respect to the alleviation of anxiety? Are the anxieties they produce actually less difficult to handle, even in the prescribed ways, than the original anxiety which they enable men to avoid? Functional theorists have not examined this question critically. We shall discuss important aspects of it in the second chapter.

[13] Homans, *op. cit.*, p. 327.

religion and society: the functionalist approach

Religion and Social Causation

Radcliffe-Brown's assertion that rites once established, together with their associated beliefs, affect behavior—that they are cause and not simply effect—leads us to further considerations. Other scholars of the world's religions have provided important insights in this regard. Among the numerous contributors, Max Weber, who wrote in the period before World War I, stands out as the great pioneer. Weber's interest in religion, comprehensive as it was, may be characterized by two strands running throughout his work. In *The Protestant Ethic and the Spirit of Capitalism*, and in his studies of the non-Christian world religions, he demonstrated the role of religion as an independent causal element influencing action throughout history. In this demonstration he sought to counteract the then-current one-sided interpretation of Marx which presented religion simply as a derivative of more fundamental social variables, an epiphenomenon with no causal significance. Weber argued that the ethic of Protestantism is antecedent to modern capitalism and that it was an important factor in its development. In his other studies, the crucial significance of religious conceptions of the human situation to the development of human societies is demonstrated.

Weber, as we have already noted, saw religion as concerned with what he called "the problem of meaning." By this term he referred to the fact that men need not only emotional adjustment but also cognitive assurance when facing the problems of suffering and death. He also had in mind the human need to understand the discrepancy between expectations and actual happenings in every society and every cultural setting. In other words, men require answers to questions concerning human destiny, the demands of morality and discipline, and the evils of injustice, suffering, and death. On the basis of a comparative study of world religions, he showed that there are several directions in which men may go to seek and work out answers to these questions. The world religions represent the working-out of different rationally integrated solutions to these problems. The problems which concerned Weber are those we have previously seen as deriving from the basic facts of the human condition: contingency, powerlessness, and scarcity. Weber shows that religions, by working out answers to these problems—answers which become part of the established culture and institutional structures of a society—affect in the most intimate way the practical attitudes of men toward various activities of daily life. In this way, religious conceptions affect the formation of goals, the rules which regulate means, and the general value structure affecting choice and decision. Weber considered that, for its adherents, religion provided an ultimate answer to the problem of meaning. But it is an answer that, through its institutionalization, enters as a causal factor in the determination of human action in varied spheres of human activity.[14]

[14] Talcott Parsons, *Essays in Sociological Theory*, rev. ed. (Glencoe, Ill.: The Free Press, 1958), pp. 208–209.

Emile Durkheim, from the period before the first World War, attempted to ask and answer two questions.[15] He was concerned first of all with what religion was, and secondly with the role it played in human society. The peculiar methodology of Durkheim [16] directed his interest to what he considered "social things," and religion was for him a "social thing" *par excellence*. He saw religion as related to a radical division of all human experience into two radically other, heterogeneous spheres. Like Malinowski (who came later), he called these the "sacred" and the "profane." The profane referred to the experience of everyday life, of which work and the workaday world was its most central and significant type case. The sacred was residual to, and other than, this workaday sphere. It lay somehow outside the profane sphere and evoked an attitude of awe and reverence. Religion was the attitude characteristic of this sacred kind of experience and was concerned, through ritual and practice, with maintaining its radical segregation from the profane.

He next raised the question of what was the object of the ritual cult, of worship, and of the attitudes of awe and reverence. Recognizing and emphasizing (in a sense overemphasizing) the social character of religion, Durkheim saw the object of religion, lurking behind the great heterogeneity of vehicles and symbols which give it concrete expression for believers, to be the group itself, society. God was the hypostatization of society, the group made into a personalized living entity. Religion was the sacralization of the traditions, embodying society's requirements for human behavior, upon which society ultimately rests. Society was greater than the individual; it gave him strength and support, and it was the source of the ideas and values which rendered his life meaningful. It made him a social being. The worship of God was seen by Durkheim as the disguised worship of society, the great entity upon which the individual depended.

From this, of course, follows the function of religion in society. Religion preserved society, kept it before men in terms of its value for them, elicited their reverence for it. In the rites of the cult the society reaffirmed itself in a symbolic acting-out of its attitudes, which by strengthening the commonly held attitudes, strengthened society itself. In Durkheim's words, ". . . before all, rites are means by which the social group reaffirms itself periodically." [17]

Although Durkheim was not primarily interested in individual phenomena, he did recognize the supportive role of religion for the believer himself: it gave the believer "impressions of comfort and dependence." [18] "The believer who has communicated with his god . . . is a man who is stronger. He feels within him more force, either to endure the trials of existence, or to conquer them." [19]

Durkheim, by emphasizing the reaffirmation of the group in the religious

[15] Émile Durkheim, *The Elementary Forms of the Religious Life*, trans. by Joseph Ward Swain (Glencoe, Ill.: The Free Press, 1954; George Allen & Unwin Ltd.).

[16] Durkheim, *The Rules of Sociological Method*, 8th ed., trans. by Sarah A. Solovay and John H. Mueller, George E. G. Catlin (ed.) (Glencoe, Ill.: The Free Press, 1950).

[17] Durkheim, *The Elementary Forms of the Religious Life*, p. 387.

[18] *Ibid.*, p. 323.

[19] *Ibid.*, p. 416.

religion and society: the functionalist approach

cult, and the sanctification of society's norms in religion itself, points out the strategic social function of religion. In another treatment he has shown how the trial and punishment of a criminal plays a ritual role analogous to religious rites: the playing out of a drama in which individuals participate vicariously. The unsocialized elements in individuals identify with the criminal and his deviant behavior; the socialized aspects of individuals identify with the forces of law and order. Both aspects of the individual are thereby involved in a drama in which the forces of law and order emerge victorious. In Durkheim's words, the spectacle acts as an agent to "heal the wounds" inflicted by the crime upon the "collective sentiments," and re-establishes the respect in which society's norms are held.[20] Similarly, religion, in its rites, elicits the acting-out of sentiments upholding fundamental norms and values and thereby re-establishes them in the consciousness of its adherents. In reciprocal reinforcements, religious beliefs sanctify norms of conduct and supply their ultimate justification, and religious rites elicit and act out attitudes expressing, and thus strengthening, the awe and respect in which such norms are held. Thus religion provides, through its sanctification and renewal of basic norms, a strategic basis for social control in the face of deviant tendencies and the expression of impulses dangerous to the stability of society.

In a criticism of Durkheim's theory, Parsons has pointed out that ". . . there is no doubt of the fundamental importance of Durkheim's insight into the exceedingly close integration of the system of religious symbols of a society and the patterns sanctioned by common moral sentiments of the members of the community." [21] Kingsley Davis, a leading functional theorist, has suggested an improvement upon Durkheim's formulation which follows Parsons' analysis. Sacred objects, instead of symbolizing society, symbolize instead the "unseen world" which "gives the actor a source and final justification for his group ends—ends that he shares with other members of his society." [22]

The Significance of Functional Theory

Let us now attempt to generalize the insights of functional theory and consider their significance for the sociological study of religion. Functional theory sees religion concerned with the aspects of experience which transcend the mundane events of everyday existence—that is, as involving belief in and a response to some kind of beyond. Hence religion becomes of sociological significance precisely in those areas of human life where knowledge and skill fail to provide the needed means of adaptation, or mechanisms of adjustment. Religion, in terms of functional theory,

[20] Durkheim, *The Division of Labor in Society*, trans. by George Simpson (Glencoe, Ill.: The Free Press, 1960), p. 108.

[21] Parsons, *op. cit.*, p. 206.

[22] Kingsley Davis, *Human Society* (New York: Macmillan Co., 1948), p. 529. We shall return in Chapter 2 to a more thorough analysis of Durkheim's treatment of the sacred.

becomes significant in connection with those elements of human experience which derive from the contingency, powerlessness, and scarcity fundamentally characteristic of the human condition. The function of religion in this connection is to provide two things. One is a larger view of a beyond, in the context of which deprivation and frustration can be experienced as meaningful. The other is the ritual means for facilitating a relationship to the beyond which gives enough security and assurance to human beings to sustain their morale. It is possible to distinguish six functions of religion in these terms.

First, religion, by its invocation of a beyond which is concerned with human destiny and welfare, and to which men may respond and relate themselves, provides *support, consolation,* and *reconciliation.* Men need emotional support in the face of uncertainty, consolation when confronted with disappointment, and reconciliation with society when alienated from its goals and norms. Defeat in the pursuit of aspirations, disappointment, and anxiety —religion provides important emotional aid in the face of these elements of the human condition. In doing this, it supports established values and goals, reinforces morale, and helps to minimize disaffection.

Second, religion offers a *transcendental relationship* through cult and the ceremonies of worship, and thereby provides the emotional ground for a new *security* and firmer *identity* amid the uncertainties and impossibilities of the human condition and the flux and change of history. Through its authoritative teaching of beliefs and values, it also provides established points of reference amid the conflicts and ambiguities of human opinions and points of view. This *priestly* function of religion contributes to stability, to order, and often to the maintenance of the status quo.

Third, religion *sacralizes the norms and values* of established society, maintaining the dominance of group goals over individual wishes, and of group disciplines over individual impulses.[23] It thereby reinforces the legitimation of the division of functions, facilities, and rewards characteristic of a given society. Moreover, since in no society do persons live up to the expectations without deviance or lapse, some method must always be found of handling the consequent alienation and guilt of the deviant individuals. Religion also performs this function by presenting ways, often ritual ways, in which *guilt can be expiated* and the individual released from his bondage to it and reintegrated into the social group. Thus religion sacralizes the norms and values, contributing to *social control;* legitimates the allocation patterns of the society, thereby aiding order and stability; and aids in the reconciliation of the disaffected.

Fourth, religion also performs a function which can be in contradiction to the previous function. Religion may also provide standards of value in terms of which institutionalized norms may be critically examined and found seriously wanting. This is especially likely to be true with respect to religions which emphasize the transcendence of God, and his consequent superiority to and independence of established authorities in society. We see this function of religion in its clearest form in the Hebrew prophets. Hence we call this the *prophetic* function. The conflicts between priestly and prophetic

[23] Davis, *op. cit.,* p. 529.

religion and society: the functionalist approach

functions of religion constitute an important aspect of the history of Biblical religion. The prophetic function is often a source of important social protest against established forms and conditions.

Fifth, religion performs important *identity* functions. We have already mentioned one aspect of these in discussing the function of the transcendental relationship involved in religion. Individuals, by their acceptance of the values involved in religion and the beliefs about human nature and destiny associated with them, develop important aspects of their own self-understanding and self-definition. Also, by their participation in religious ritual and worship, they act out significant elements of their own identity. In these ways, religion affects individuals' understanding of *who they are* and *what they are*. Davis has written that "religion gives the individual a sense of identity with the distant past and the limitless future. It expands his ego by making his spirit significant for the universe and the universe significant for him." [24] In periods of rapid social change and large-scale social mobility, the contribution of religion to identity may become greatly enhanced. For example, Will Herberg, in his sociological study of American religion in the 1950's, suggests that one important way in which Americans establish their identity is by being members of one of the "three religions of democracy," Protestantism, Catholicism, or Judaism.[25]

Sixth, religion is related to the growth and maturation of the individual and his passage through the various age gradings distinguished by his society. Psychologists have shown that individual growth passes through a series of encounters characteristic of the various age levels of men, a series of encounters from infancy to death. In each of these, new problems challenge the individual. In infancy, one must learn some degree of basic trust in other human beings; later one must develop some ability to function autonomously, to stand on one's own feet; and later still one must learn to defer satisfactions and to discipline impulses in the pursuit of socially approved ends. Religion sacralizes norms and ends; it supports the disciplines of society in important respects; it offers support in uncertainty, consolation in disappointment and defeat; it contributes to the developing identity of the individual. Obviously, in all these ways it involves itself in the learning process. But does religion support and encourage maturation, the development of autonomy, and self-direction? Or does it provide a too-authoritarian and over-protective setting which inhibits maturation and tends to keep individuals dependent upon religious institutions? The *relation of religion to maturation*—or, as it is called, religion's *maturation function*—must be studied specifically for specific religions at particular times and places. It is

---

[24] Davis, *op. cit.*, pp. 531, 532–533. Davis also states: "In these ways religion contributes to the integration of the personality. But like other medicines it can sometimes make worse the very thing it seeks to remedy. Innumerable are the psychoses and neuroses that have a religious content. The supraempirical world is so elastic, so susceptible to manipulation by the imagination, that the disordered mind can seize upon it to spin itself into almost any kind of bizarre pattern. It is a prop which takes courage to do without but which one dares not lean on too heavily" (p. 533). This is a statement of functional significance deserving lengthier study and treatment.

[25] Will Herberg, *Protestant, Catholic, Jew* (Garden City, N. Y.: Doubleday, 1955).

15

a subject that needs much more careful study before anything definitive may be said concerning it.

Religion, then, in the view of functional theory, identifies the individual with his group, supports him in uncertainty, consoles him in disappointment, attaches him to society's goals, enhances his morale, and provides him with elements of identity. It acts to reinforce the unity and stability of society by supporting social control, enhancing established values and goals, and providing the means for overcoming guilt and alienation. It may also perform a prophetic role and prove itself an unsettling or even subversive influence in any particular society.

The contributions of religion to society may be either positive or negative—they may support its continued existence, or they may play a part in undermining it. Functional theory has been criticized because of its basic assumption that all surviving elements in a society must perform a predominantly positive function. It is a justified criticism. It has been noted that functionalists have usually ". . . concentrated upon those *positive functions* which are *not usually known* to the members of society, i.e., the positive, latent functions. The rebels and debunkers among modern economists and historians have concentrated upon the *negative latent functions*. It is clear that much exploration remains to be done. . . ." concerning manifest functions of both a positive and negative character.[26]

J. Milton Yinger, an American sociologist of religion, has discussed the difficulties involved in the functionalist approach. One is its tendency to assume that social systems are completely integrated and that all elements are functional and indispensable.[27] He also considers the effects of other factors upon the efficacy with which religion performs an integrating function, as well as the fact that religion can also be a disturbing and revolutionary element.[28]

Functional theory provides one fruitful pathway or access to understanding religion as a universal social phenomenon. It has called our attention to a strategic aspect of all religions: their transcendent reference and its functional significance for culture, society, and human personality. Religion provides culture with an anchorage point, beyond empirical proof or disproof, in terms of which ultimate meaning is postulated. This ultimate meaning provides a ground for the goals and aspirations of men, thereby evoking an attitude of awe which ensures continuing and effective agreement with the values and goals of the culture itself. Religion contributes to social systems in that at the breaking points, when men face contingency and powerlessness, it offers an answer to the problem of meaning. It also provides a means for adjusting to the frustrations involved in disappointment, whether this derives from the human condition or the institutional arrangements of the society. The function of religion for human personalities is that it sup-

---

[26] W. J. Goode, *Religion Among the Primitives* (Glencoe, Ill.: The Free Press, 1951), p. 33.

[27] J. Milton Yinger, *Religion, Society and the Individual* (New York: Macmillan Co., 1957), pp. 58–59, *passim*.

[28] *Ibid.*, pp. 66 ff.

16

religion and society: the functionalist approach

plies the basic ground guaranteeing the meaningfulness of human life and effort, and offers an outlet for expressive needs and a catharsis and consolation for human emotions. It likewise supports human discipline by its sanctification of the norms and rules of society, and thereby plays a part both in socializing the individual and in maintaining social stability.

Important as the functional approach is—and it is of great significance as a conceptual tool in understanding the relation between religion and society—its approach to the study of religion is partial and incomplete. Many significant questions about religion are neither raised nor answered within its purview. Also, it tends to emphasize the conservative functions of religion and neglects its creative and potentially revolutionary character. This is especially the case when the functional questions are approached within the context of analysis of the social system, rather than in terms of an analysis of action as in the early work of Parsons.[29] In the context of the social system, functional theory would seem to imply that religion is a functional necessity in all societies and that groups in societies that oppose religion are simply "mistaken." Thus functional theory lends itself to an "apologetic" distortion, despite the conviction of its practitioners that this is not the case.[30]

In relation to this curious bias, functional theory may also be said to neglect the process of the secularization of culture, perhaps the most significant development of the last several hundred years, and its functional or dysfunctional significance for human societies. In our age of turmoil and transition this is a serious omission, indeed. If religion is a functionally necessary myth from which only the elite can escape, but which is necessary for the mass of mankind, a functional problem of the first order is posed. The opinion of Kingsley Davis is palpably inadequate: "The tendency toward secularization probably cannot continue to the point where religion entirely disappears. Secularization will likely be terminated by religious revivals of one sort or another." [31] Yinger, however, recognizes that there are "secular alternatives" to religion, a fact which interested Max Weber, who spoke of the role of "religion surrogates" in secularized societies. Yinger makes the important point that, from a functional point of view, "religion—non-religion is a continuum," [32] and points out the quasi-religious character of some secular movements—for example, in his treatment of the "religious aspects of communism." [33] Yet, while functional theorists have recognized the existence of functional equivalents of religion (secular and at times formally anti-religious in character), insufficient research has been done in this area.

Functional theory, like all sociological theory concerning religion, strives to maintain an attitude of value-freedom. It makes no judgment as to the ultimate truth or falsity of religious beliefs. Like all sociology, it takes a so-

[29] Talcott Parsons, *The Structure of Social Action*, 2nd ed. (Glencoe, Ill.: The Free Press, 1949), especially Part III on Max Weber.
[30] Kingsley Davis, "The Myth of Functional Analysis as a Special Method in Sociology and Anthropology," *American Sociological Review* (December 1959), 24:766.
[31] Davis, *Human Society*, pp. 544–545.
[32] Yinger, *op. cit.*, p. 118.
[33] *Ibid.*, p. 120.

17

called "naturalistic approach" to religion. As a social science, sociology seeks to understand behavior in terms of natural causes and effects. This is not an anti-religious ideological position, since even causes beyond nature, if they act upon men, must act through men and the nature of men. Modern Biblical research, even when conducted in an orthodox religious frame of reference, has completely recognized this as the basis of its methodology. It is a necessary axiom for the pursuit of scientific study in any field of inquiry. Yet, while acting rightly in avoiding value judgments about faith and doubt, functional theorists are not justified in neglecting an examination of the functional significance of doubt itself, and the reasons for its appearance in certain societies and certain periods of history. Doubt, as well as belief, is subject to social conditioning and, like belief, has positive or negative functional significance.

One of the most significant contributions of functional theory is that it has called our attention to that characteristic of religion which offers us another starting point from which to begin the sociological study of religion from a complementary perspective. Functional theory has emphasized the importance of "breaking points," where everyday thought and action are transcended in human experience. It has thus directed our attention to that experience which is the source of the human response we call religion. As Malinowski has stated, "Human organism reacts to this [the "breaking point"] in spontaneous outbursts, in which rudimentary modes of behavior and rudimentary beliefs in their efficiency are engendered." [34] This fact, which is the central and strategic insight of functional theory, points out to us the centrality of the problem of just what is the experience at the "breaking points" which gives rise to religion as a human phenomenon. Moreover, functional theorists such as Durkheim and his followers have pointed out where to begin our search for the answer to this question. They have done this by calling our attention to the special character of religious phenomena: their concern with the sacred. The question arises in the context of functional theory: What is the religious experience, and how are rites and beliefs and social institutions engendered out of it?

[34] Malinowski, *op. cit.*, p. 90.

religion and society: the functionalist approach

the religious
experience

two

In the first chapter we came to understand something of the part played by religion in the functioning of human societies, and of its contribution to the economy of individual personalities. We saw that religion was related to crucial breaking points in human experience. Moreover, we saw that experience at these breaking points, which we called religious, was characterized by a special quality eliciting intense respect—that it was an experience of "the sacred." On the basis of these insights, the question arises: Is not religion itself an experience of some kind of fundamental breaking point? We must now look more closely both at the concept of the sacred and the idea of the breaking point.

The Sacred, the Extraordinary, and the Phenomenon of Charisma

We shall examine the idea of the sacred in the works of two men who have written classic books on the subject: Emile Durkheim, and the German religious scholar, Rudolf Otto.[1] Durkheim saw religion pre-

[1] Emile Durkheim, *The Elementary Forms of the Religious Life*, trans. by Joseph Ward Swain (Glencoe, Ill.: The Free Press, 1954; George Allen & Unwin Ltd.); Rudolf Otto, *The Idea of the Holy*, 2nd ed., trans. by J. W. Harvey (London: Oxford University Press, 1950).

19

supposing a classification of all the contents of human experience into two absolutely opposed categories, the sacred and the profane. The profane is the realm of routine experience, coinciding to a considerable degree with what Pareto called "logico-experimental" experience, which is transcended by religion. It is the sphere of adaptive behavior. The sphere of the sacred is, as we have seen from Malinowski and others, entirely other than this utilitarian sphere. Durkheim states that the sacred is superior to the profane in dignity and expresses a superior seriousness. Religion as an attitude toward the sacred has no end or purpose extrinsic to itself. The attitude elicited by the symbols which represent the sacred is one of intense respect. It is, as the great phenomenologist of religion, van der Leeuw, has said, one of *awe*. This may be seen not simply in human behavior in the presence of such symbols, but also in the fact that sacred things are always set apart by interdictions and isolated by ritual practices. Religious rites are not performed primarily to achieve something but to express an attitude. In Van der Leeuw's words, *awe*, once established, "develops into *observance*." [2] Thus there arises in the experience of the sacred an attitude and a set of practices. In William James' words, religion is a matter of "feelings, acts and experiences," and, out of these, "theologies, philosophies, and ecclesiastical organizations may secondarily grow." [3]

Durkheim describes seven additional characteristics of the sacred as something experienced by and affecting human beings. First of all, the sacred as an aspect of what is experienced involves a recognition of or a belief in *power* or *force*. It is not to symbols or to other objects that religious cult is primarily addressed but to a power spread through such things. Powers, or forces, lie at the root of the religious attitude. Second, the sacred is characterized by *ambiguity*; it is a matter of ambiguous power or powers. There are two aspects of this ambiguity. Sacred things and forces are ambiguous in that they are both physical *and* moral, human *and* cosmic or natural, positive *and* negative, propitious *and* unpropitious, attractive *and* repugnant, helpful *and* dangerous to men.

Three closely related characteristics of the sacred discussed by Durkheim are to be seen in the fact that the sacred is *non-utilitarian, non-empirical*, and *does not involve knowledge*. Utility and everydayness are foreign to the sacred, and work is the eminent form of profane activity. Durkheim stated that the sacred quality is not intrinsic to objects but is conferred on them by religious thought and feeling. The sacred is not an aspect of empirical nature but rather is superimposed upon it. Moreover, it is an aspect which does not in a useful manner aid our acting upon natural forces and things. The sacred is not a matter of knowledge based on the experience of the senses.

A sixth characteristic of the sacred described by Durkheim is its supportive and strength-giving character. Sacred forces act upon believers and

[2] G. Van der Leeuw, *Religion In Essence and Manifestation*, Vol. I (New York: Harper Torchbooks, 1963), p. 49.
[3] William James, *The Varieties of Religious Experience* (New York: The Modern Library, Random House, n.d.), p. 32.

20

worshipers to strengthen and sustain them. The religious attitude exalts the believer and raises him above himself. A seventh characteristic of the sacred is that it makes a demand on the believer and worshiper. It impinges on human consciousness with moral obligation, with an ethical imperative. The sacred, then, in terms of Durkheim's analysis is radically other than the profane; is non-utilitarian and non-empirical; does not involve knowledge but involves power; is ambiguous with respect to nature, culture, and human welfare; is strength-giving and sustaining; elicits intense respect and makes an ethical demand upon the believer.

Rudolf Otto, in his book *The Idea of the Holy*, analyzed the sacred or holy in terms which he considered more fundamental than those to be found in the German Protestant theology of his day. He felt that rationalism had affected religious thinking by reducing the idea of the holy to those aspects of God which could be conceptualized and expressed in intellectual terms. Moreover, he pointed out the tendency of religion in the West to confuse the original idea of the holy with ethical conceptions and to see the holy as somehow synonymous with the "completely good" or the "absolute good." It was Otto's position that this confusion, while not unrelated to the *original* meaning of the holy, represents an historical development of that original meaning, the "gradual shaping and filling in with ethical meaning, or what we shall call the 'schematization,' of what was a unique feeling-response, which can in itself be ethically neutral and claims consideration in its own right." The holy, or "numinous," to use the term Otto has coined, is something beyond rational and ethical conceptions. He points out that in the three languages strategic to the transmission of the Western religious tradition, the terms *qadôsh* (Hebrew), *ayios* (Greek), and *sanctus* or *sacer* (Latin) refer to the "real innermost core" of all religion. The holy is a "pre-eminently living force." It involves for Otto an irreducible category of experience, a given element of data, a specific feeling-response. What is involved is a "mystery and above all creatures," something "hidden and esoteric," which we can "experience in feelings." The holy is "the *mysterium tremendum et fascinosum*." It is "wholly other," that which "is quite beyond the sphere of the usual, the intelligible, and the familiar. . . ." What is involved is might, absolute power, and the "element of majesty or absolute overpoweringness" elicits in the believer a feeling of "creature consciousness," the "raw material for the feelings of religious humility." The *mysterium tremendum* involves the "urgency" or "energy" of the numinous object.

What is involved is something "whose kind and character are incommensurable with our own," which evokes "a peculiar dread," but is at the same time attractive and inviting to the beholder. "These two qualities, the daunting and the fascinating, now combine in a strange harmony of contrasts, and the resultant [is the] dual character of the numinous consciousness. . . ." Also according to Otto, the experience of the holy arouses a feeling of unworthiness in the believer.[4]

The coincidence of many strategic elements in the analyses of Durk-

---

[4] Otto, *op. cit., passim.*

heim's and Otto's treatment of the sacred or holy is worthy of our attention. These elements are the extraordinary character of the phenomenon, its implication of power, its ambiguity in relation to man, its awesome character and the feeling of dependence it arouses. It should also be noted that what Durkheim refers to as "the implication of obligation" is closely related to what Otto describes as "the sense of unworthiness."

Other students have also pointed out the basic characteristics described by Otto and Durkheim. Van der Leeuw, in his phenomenological study, emphasizes power and the arousal of awe, as well as the attractive and forbidding aspects of the sacred. He points to the radical contrast between the unusual and the powerful, and the ordinary and everyday. Robert Lowie, the American anthropologist, spoke of the sacred or religious sphere as that of the "extraordinary," in contrast with an everyday sphere of the "ordinary." [5] The British anthropologist, R. R. Marett, saw religion concerned with the "extraordinary" as contrasted with the workaday. Long ago, Plato summed up the extraordinary and strength-giving aspects of religion:

> But the gods, taking pity on mankind, born to work, laid down the succession of recurring feasts to restore them from their fatigue, and gave them the Muses, and Apollo their leader, and Dionysus, as companions in their feasts, so that nourishing themselves in festive companionship with the gods, they should again stand upright and erect.

A Swiss scholar, Edmund Rochdieu, speaks of a "complex structure of the religious sentiment which accompanies dependence upon the sacred." In this he invokes again the same kind of ambiguity stressed by Durkheim and Otto. The sacred arouses feelings which are simultaneously characterized by terror and attraction, fear and love, horror and fascination; and there accompanies these feelings a conviction in the believer that he is somehow caught up and enveloped in an overarching destiny.[6] It is quite obvious that all these analyses point to a characteristic breaking point with the ordinary or workaday world, a point which is central to religious experience.

In Max Weber's treatment of *charisma*, we see the intimate relationship of this phenomenon with what Durkheim has called the sacred and Otto the holy. In charisma we see a definite breaking point in the world of everydayness, one closely connected with an unusual person and involving obligation. Weber defines charisma as "*. . . a certain quality of an individual personality by virtue of which he is set apart from ordinary men and treated as endowed with supernatural, superhuman, or at least specifically exceptional powers or qualities. These are such as are not accessible to the ordinary person, but are regarded as of divine origin or as exemplary, and on the basis of them the individual concerned is treated as a leader.*" [7] For Weber, charisma

[5] Robert Lowie, *Primitive Religion* (New York: Boni & Liveright, 1924), pp. xv ff and 338 ff.

[6] Edmund Rochdieu, "Affective Dynamism and Religious Sentiment," *Cross Currents* (Spring–Summer 1954), 4: 223–235.

[7] Max Weber, *The Theory of Social and Economic Organization*, trans. by A. M. Henderson and Talcott Parsons, Talcott Parsons (ed.) (New York: Oxford University Press, 1947), pp. 358–359.

the religious experience

played two significant roles in human society. As out-of-the-ordinary, it was a source of instability and innovation, and hence a strategic element in social change. In its elicitation of followers and its evocation of respect, it was the source of that element in authority which renders it voluntarily respected, accepted, and followed. Charismatic phenomena, though associated with actual persons, convey to the beholder who is sensitive to their appeal, supraempirical aspects and implications. Charisma issues a call, and those who for whatever reasons can hear this call respond with conviction. These followers feel that "it is the *duty* of those who have been called to a charismatic mission to recognize its quality and to act accordingly." Charismatic leadership is "specifically outside the realm of everyday routine and the profane sphere." It is *extraordinary* as opposed to the *everyday, sacred* in contrast to the *profane.*[8] Like Otto's treatment of the holy as beyond ethical considerations, Weber's analysis of charisma finds it ethically neutral. Like Durkheim's treatment of the sacred, which sees its opposite in the world of work, Weber's analysis finds charisma as "specifically foreign to economic considerations." Pure charisma is alien to the established institutions of society. "From a substantive point of view, every charismatic authority would have to subscribe to the proposition, 'It is written . . . , but I say unto you. . . .' "[9]

Charismatic phenomena are unstable and temporary and can prolong their existence only by becoming routinized—that is, by becoming transformed or incorporating themselves into the routine institutionalized structures of society. Such routinization may develop either in a rational and bureaucratic or a traditional direction, and there thus arise traditional and rational authority in different societies. It is this charismatic element, carried over into established social structures, which becomes the basis for the legitimation of established authority. Here Weber points to the function of the sacred in social control: the reinforcement of society's norms and its structures of authority. Legitimacy is seen as derived from a "transcendental reference" which originates in the charismatic experience and is carried over in the evolution of social structures out of that experience. The founded religions, which issue in specifically religious organizations, as distinguished from the sacralization of "natural groups" such as the family and the community,[10] derive from the experience of followers with charismatic leaders. They are derived from a particular kind of experience of the sacred embodied in unusual men.

There are three chief characteristics which are descriptive of charisma in all of Weber's treatment. Charisma is *unusual*, radically different from the routine and the everyday; it is *spontaneous* in contrast to stable, established social forms; and it is a source of new forms and new movements, and hence *creative* in a fundamental sociological sense. It is interesting to note that these three characteristics coincide remarkably with the attributes which

---

[8] See Talcott Parsons, *The Structure of Social Action* (Glencoe, Ill.: The Free Press, 1949), Chap. 17, pp. 658 ff.

[9] Weber, *op. cit., passim.*

[10] Joachim Wach, *The Sociology of Religion* (Chicago: University of Chicago Press, 1944), Chap. 4, pp. 54–108.

theologians in the Judeo-Christian and Islamic traditions have attributed to God. God is seen as radically different from his creation—"wholly other," to use Otto's term. He is seen as "the living God" in the terms of biblical theology, and in theologies affected by Aristotelian concepts as "Pure Act" (Actus Purus) in whom there is nothing unrealized, who has neither past nor future, but whose life is an eternal present, an infinite "now." And he is the creator of all other beings.

In this examination of the sacred or holy, and of the phenomenon of charisma, we have actually been examining an important aspect of the religious experience. In the religious experience men respond to the unusual, to power, to spontaneity, to creativity. Their response is characterized by intense respect and great attraction. Out of this religious experience stable forms of thought, feeling, action, and relationship evolve. We have taken a first step in understanding the religious experience—an experience of the sacred or holy—and the typical response which men have made to it: respect and fascination. In this way we have begun the consideration of that breaking point which lies at the core of religion.

The Sacred and Ultimacy

The sacred indicates a power which, though it manifests itself in experience, lies beyond it, and the religious experience is an experience of this power. The religious experience is a response to things or events experienced as sacred—that is, as a revelation of power eliciting a specific kind of response which combines both intense respect and strong attraction. What kind of object or what kind of event conveys this impression of power and elicits this specific mode of response? Our analysis of charisma has suggested three characteristics: unusualness, spontaneity, and creativity. All these suggest things or events which are "outside" the everyday and routine experiences of life.

Two further questions arise for our understanding of the religious experience. First, what kinds of objects and events are involved as bearers or symbols of the power which is the object of the experience? And, since the sacred or the charismatic is attractive and involves obligation from those who respond to it, there arises a second, even a third, question: Why does power apperceived in the mode of sacredness issue a call to the believer? Why do human beings enter into a relationship with sacred things? We shall consider these questions in the light of the contributions of five important scholars.

Max Müller, an important late-nineteenth-century student of religion, saw the unpredictable in nature—the cosmic unknown—which he characterized as "the infinite," as one important root of religion.[11] Durkheim rejects this proposition in his attempt to establish a purely social origin of religion. We have already seen, however, that religion is in part a response to problems

---

[11] See Durkheim, op. cit., pp. 72 ff.

which involve uncertainty and powerlessness, and it can hardly be denied that man's experience of both has long involved dramatic (and often traumatic) natural happenings—famines, floods, epidemics, hurricanes, and tornadoes. Such events seem most appropriate to serve as agents revealing to men the power or powers that lie beneath the calm surface of ordinary experience. They seem ideally suited to act as epiphanies of power, and a comparative study of religion shows that indeed they do.

Durkheim himself pointed out that the sacred forces appeared as both cosmic and social, but his explanation that the cosmic or natural objects or events serve simply to symbolize social power is one-sided and partial. Man is a part of nature and his destiny is involved in nature's processes and events. Of the powers which act upon him, the natural are as impressive as the social. The aborigines studied by Durkheim saw the sacred forces as animating living things, expressing themselves in their reproduction as well as infusing the human society and expressing themselves in its solidarity. Moreover, sophisticated theologies develop this simpler feeling about a power at once cosmic or natural and social and moral, by characterizing God as the creator of nature as well as the source of spiritual and moral goodness. Van der Leeuw points out that not only the unusual in nature, not simply the dramatic and unexpected, but also "a manifestation of immutably ordered regularity"[12] can become a revelation of power—the power that lies behind ordinary things—in van der Leeuw's words, the power of "the sacred world above." Hence, a power that is beyond the appearances of everyday things and events may be apperceived by men in both their experience of the unusual and of the established. Weber has shown that, despite the loss of spontaneity involved in the routinization of charisma, a charismatic element remains as central to the institutions of the established social order. Similarly, van der Leeuw has shown that the established order of nature, as well as its unpredictable spontaneities to be seen in unusual events, may also serve to convey to men the impression of a power beyond and behind ordinary appearances.

Another important student of religion, N. D. Fustel de Coulanges, in his great classic pioneer work, *The Ancient City*, speaks of two sources of religion.[13] One of these is *internal*, born of the psychological projections of men and expressing the subjective precipitates of their experience. The second is derived from an *external* source, from the reactions of men to natural forces. Religion is concerned with a power or powers—Otto's *mysterium tremendum*—which lies behind both the interior and exterior, the objective and the subjective, aspects of reality experienced by men. It is directed to a potency from which both man's external and internal worlds are derived. Although catastrophe and misfortune may plague men, religion refers all their confusion and disappointment to a deeper ground of existence, in terms of which it all makes sense.

An American anthropologist, Edward Sapir, in a penetrating analysis of

[12] Van der Leeuw, *op. cit.*, p. 71.
[13] N. D. Fustel de Coulanges, *The Ancient City* (Garden City, N.Y.: Doubleday, 1950).

25

the religious experience

the human meaning of religion, has pointed out that the essence of religion is to be found in "man's never-ceasing attempt to discover a road to spiritual serenity across the perplexities and dangers of daily life." Conceding the cultural and individual relativity involved in the definition of spiritual serenity, Sapir points out that for all societies and individuals the essence of religion lies in "the haunting realization of ultimate powerlessness in an inscrutable world, and the unquestioning and thoroughly irrational conviction of the possibility of gaining mystic security by somehow identifying oneself with what can never be known."

> Religion is omnipresent fear and a vast humility paradoxically turned into bedrock security, for once the fear is imaginatively taken to one's heart and the humility confessed for good and all, the triumph of human consciousness is assured. There can be neither fear nor humiliation for deeply religious natures, for they have intuitively experienced both of these emotions in advance of the declared hostility of an overwhelming world, coldly indifferent to human desire. . . . It is the pursuit, conscious or unconscious, of ultimate reality following total and necessary defeat that constitutes the core of religion.[14]

Sapir directs our attention to man's aloneness and powerlessness at the crucial breaking points where he confronts an inscrutable world. Beneath the institutionalized relationships of society and the definitions of existence and value of culture, there remains the "hostility of an overwhelming world, coldly indifferent to human desire." Sapir states that men handle this confrontation by gaining "mystic security" through an *identification* with "what can never be known." Men attempt to enter into a relationship with what lies behind the experienced world. Sapir suggests that man's identity and selfhood is threatened by the impact of contingency and powerlessness upon him, but that in the religious response—in the identification with the power that lies behind and beyond appearances—"the triumph of human consciousness is assured" and fear is turned into "bedrock security." Sapir suggests that human consciousness is a frail thing facing an overwhelming, a dangerous, an indifferent world, and this confrontation threatens to be shattering to the structure of consciousness itself. It is a paradox of human consciousness that, frail though it be, it can proceed beyond accepted definitions to a breaking point which threatens its very structure. As Pascal has said, "Man is a reed, but he is a thinking reed." One important element of this religious experience is that it involves man's attempt to respond to and enter into a relationship with what lies behind appearance. It is a human response at the "limit-situation"—where man breaks through to some kind of beyond.

We must not think of this experience of man at the limit-situation as simply a philosophical experience, an experience of thought. Philosophy attempts to convert this limit-situation into intellectual concepts which can be handled relatively free of the burden of anxiety originally involved. Sapir is referring to a more immediate and more holistic experience—an unreflective

---

[14] Edward Sapir, *Culture, Language and Personality* (Berkeley: University of California Press, 1960), pp. 122–123.

the religious experience

confrontation by the whole man. The philosophical experience and the experience we are attempting to understand, however, have this in common: life, with its events at breaking points, and thought, with its capacity to question and surpass its own formulations, propel man beyond accepted and accustomed answers to significant questions. In both act and thought, man goes beyond ideas which are less-than-ultimate; he is propelled toward ultimacy. Hence an important element of the religious experience is that it is concerned with the ultimate. The experience of the sacred is, as we have seen from the start, an experience of a beyond. It is an experience of ultimacy. The power or powers revealed to the believer are ultimate powers. In developed theologies they are conceptualized as the Ultimate Power.

Religion is man's response to breaking points at which he experiences ultimate and sacred power. Out of this experience religious organizations, ritual practices, and belief and values evolve. Such institutionalized religious forms express the human answer engendered at the breaking points while putting men into ritual relationship with sacred and ultimate powers. Here we catch the first glimpse of a fundamental instability which exists at the heart of all institutionalized religion, an instability we must consider in detail in later chapters. Life and thought propel men to the limit-situation, push them to breaking points that go beyond established relationships and accepted answers to significant questions. Although religions emerge out of such experiences and responses, and embody the answers evolved in such confrontations, religion once established does not provide secure and permanent answers. Life and thought continue to drive men beyond the established institutionalized answers and their representation in religious forms. *Doubt* comes into existence as a fundamental breaking point within the religious context itself.

Sapir has shown us that men are capable of proceeding toward ultimacy; men desire ultimate answers to the problem of meaning and wish to enter into relationship with an ultimate ground of existence and value. Moreover, both the conditions of life and the implications of man's thinking drive men toward ultimacy. There is thus created a situation in which everything apparently stable, including human consciousness itself, can be threatened. Religion is a response to the ultimate which becomes institutionalized in thought, practice, and organization. Established religion, by institutionalizing answers and mechanisms of adjustment at the limit-situation—a breaking point involving ultimacy—is able to perform the functions in support of social stability and personal adjustment indicated by functional theory. But institutionalized religion itself rests upon an unstable base, since it is vulnerable to that form of breakthrough known in religious language as *doubt*. The "bedrock security" which Sapir saw deriving from a relationship to the beyond is itself subject to fissure.

The renowned contemporary theologian, Paul Tillich, has emphasized the centrality of the encounter with ultimacy in the religious experience.[15]

15 See especially Paul Tillich, *Biblical Religion and the Search for Ultimate Reality* (Chicago: University of Chicago Press, 1955), and *The Courage to Be* (New Haven: Yale University Press, 1959).

He compares the way in which ultimacy is met in both the intellectual or philosophical experience and in the religious experience. In our intellectual examination of reality, our philosophical analysis of being, ". . . we are driven from one level to another to a point where we cannot speak of level anymore, where we must ask for that which is the ground of all levels, giving them their structure and their power of being." [16] In religion, however, we do not simply come into contact with *things*. We do not simply meet "objects of a cognitive approach but elements of an encounter, namely the encounter with the holy. They are parts of this encounter, not as things or values, but as bearers of something beyond themselves. This something beyond themselves is the holy, the numinous presence of that which concerns us ultimately." [17] Here Tillich brings together the two conceptions we saw in Durkheim and Otto, and in Sapir. The holy is the ultimate, experienced not simply intellectually but as part of a personal encounter. As a Christian theologian, Tillich sees the holy involving a person-to-person relationship to God. Religion for Tillich "deals with what concerns us inescapably, ultimately, unconditionally." [18]

What our examination of the religious experience has revealed so far is this: The religious experience is an encounter with a beyond, with a power beyond the appearances of things and events, with an ultimate power seen as ground of existence. Such an ultimate ground of being is experienced through empirical things and events; it is experienced as sacred—that is, as eliciting intense awe and exercising a strong attraction. We have also seen that out of the religious experience, beliefs, practices, and religious organizations evolve, answering basic questions through their belief systems and providing means of adjustment through a relationship to the beyond. But these institutional patterns are not ultimate in their attempt to institutionalize an answer to ultimate problems. Within the context of established religion, doubt arises. There arises at this point the fundamental question: What is actually involved in the religious experience: reality or illusion? In discussing this question, we shall consider the contributions of four quite different investigators: Martin Buber, Georg Simmel, Ludwig Feuerbach, and Sigmund Freud.

Ultimacy, Meaning, and Relationship

Martin Buber points out that man's relationship to his world is not limited to a *technical* relationship; it is not simply that of a maker of things and a manipulator of natural forces. Manipulation and control do not exhaust the ways in which human beings exist within their environments. Human beings also enter into a form of commerce with their world which is of a more thoroughly relational character. Both with respect to persons, and to their situation generally, men take a stand "in relation to" an other, or others. Buber calls the technical relation an *I-It* relation and the

[16] Tillich, *Biblical Religion and the Search for Ultimate Reality*, pp. 12–13.
[17] *Ibid.*, pp. 24–25.
[18] Paul Tillich, *The Protestant Era*, trans. by James Luther Adams (Chicago: University of Chicago Press, 1948), p. 87.

the religious experience

other an *I-Thou* relation. Moreover, it is his contention that the I-Thou relation is primary in human experience.[19]

The realm in which the I-Thou relation may be most plainly seen is, of course, in the relationships among human beings themselves. But this mode of response is not confined to this sphere alone. Buber has shown that it is a mode of relationship characteristic of man's relationship to the non-human world as well. The Frankforts, *et al.*, in their treatment of the religions of ancient Egypt and Mesopotamia, show that in archaic cultures men tended to respond fundamentally in terms of an I-Thou relation to the total situation in which they found themselves.

> The ancients, like the modern savages, saw man always as part of society, and society as imbedded in nature and dependent upon cosmic forces. For them nature and man did not stand in opposition and did not, therefore, have to be apprehended by different modes of cognition. . . . The fundamental differences between the attitudes of modern and ancient man as regards the surrounding world is this: for modern, scientific man the phenomenal world is primarily an "It"; for ancient—and also for primitive— man it is a "Thou."

In ancient cultures the "whole man confronts a living 'Thou' in nature; and the whole man—emotional and imaginative, as well as intellectual—gives expression to the experience." [20] Buber states that man in the I-Thou relation responds to a "Presence," and that the I-Thou of religion is a relationship to this Presence. This presence lies beyond appearances; it is not empirically known either in terms of scientific or ordinary common-sense knowledge.

Georg Simmel points out that in religion we have the heightening and isolation of elements of everyday attitudes and relationships. He emphasizes that science is "a heightening, a refinement, a completion," of methods of knowing used in practical life; that art is a similar isolation and heightening of aesthetic elements found in ordinary experience. Similarly, in religion, faith is "first a relation between individuals." The "peculiar admixture of unselfish surrender and fervent desire, of humility and exaltation, of sensual concreteness and spiritual abstraction, which occasion a certain degree of emotional tension" that is central to religion, is found "in many other relations . . . with more or less strength, now appearing merely like a light overtone, and again as a quite distinct coloring." In religion certain aspects of human relationships are isolated, concentrated on a supraempirical presence or beyond, and regarded as normative.[21] Thus Simmel underlines two important aspects of religion. First of all, religion is, as we have already discovered, a matter of relationship. Second, in forming religious relationships, men tend to model their relation to God, to gods, to supernatural forces or any other conceptualizations of the beyond, on the existing social relations

[19] Martin Buber, *I and Thou*, 2nd ed., trans. by Ronald Gregor Smith (New York: Scribner's, 1958).
[20] Henri Frankfort, Mrs. Henri Frankfort, John A. Wilson, and Thorkild Jacobsen, *Before Philosophy* (Harmondsworth, Middlesex: Penguin Books, 1949), pp. 12–14.
[21] Georg Simmel, "A Contribution to the Sociology of Religion," trans. by W. W. Elwang, *American Journal of Sociology* (May 1955), Part II, 60:2–14.

29

of their society, expressing attitudes and feelings already present in normal everyday relationships. This reveals to us one important way in which religion —both religious ritual practices expressing attitudes, and religious ideas conceptualizing beliefs—is influenced by its social milieu. Men will tend to enter into relationships with the sacred in terms of the kinds of relationships which have become second nature to them in their society. And the attitude of respect for the sacred will be an intensification of the kinds of respect found in other social relationships.

All religious thought, of course, once it reaches a level of sophistication, recognizes that the reality of the presence encountered in the beyond is a supraempirical matter, not subject to generally accepted empirical proof. Moreover, sophisticated Western theology casts its definition in terms of analogical concepts taken from everyday language and attributed to God in analogy only. Hence such theologies admit, so to speak, that important aspects of their ideas are socially and culturally conditioned. Belief in the supraempirical involves faith; definition by analogy involves projection of here-and-now characteristics into the beyond.

We have seen that the religious response involves relationship, and that relationship in the religious experience is modeled after more ordinary relationships in the society. But the elements of faith and projection found in the religious response raise again the question that we posed at the beginning of this discussion: What is the object of the religious relation? Does man respond to a real outside presence or does he simply project interior psychic phenomena?

The Problem of Projection

According to Ludwig Feuerbach, the true content of religion, or of the conception of God, is anthropological; religion is the projection of human nature into the beyond. "Religion is man's earliest . . . indirect form of self knowledge."

> Man—this is the mystery of religion—projects his being into objectivity, and then again makes himself an object to this projected image of himself thus converted into a subject; . . . God is the highest subjectivity of man abstracted from himself. . . .[22]

Feuerbach calls our attention to the elements of projection in religious conceptions. He sees man alienated from himself and thereby damaged in his self-fulfillment by such projection. A similar understanding of religious thought has been advanced by an American sociologist, T. H. Grafton, who, following George H. Mead, Charles Cooley, and John Dewey, sees the "supernatural" as the "other," which man creates in order to respond to it.[23] The position of Feuerbach resembles that of Durkheim in one important respect: Both see the ideational content of religion as a projection of man.

[22] Ludwig Feuerbach, *The Essence of Christianity*, trans. by George Eliot (New York: Harper, 1957), pp. 13, 14, 29–30, 31.
[23] T. H. Grafton, "Religious Origins and Sociological Theory," *American Sociological Review* (December 1941), 10:726–739.

the religious experience

Durkheim, however, introduces and emphasizes the sociological dimension. God represents the hypostatization of society, which supports man's morale but also impinges upon him as something other—in Durkheim's terms, with "exteriority" and "constraint." Feuerbach sees this projective process as a source of man's alienation from himself and consequently as making man unable to accept and develop his own natural endowment.

Our analysis to this point has disclosed several important elements in the religious experience and has revealed to us some idea of how these elements are interrelated. The religious experience is an experience at the breaking point, at what can be called the limit-situation, where man, propelled either by thought or by the events of life, breaks through the here-and-now. At the limit-situation, man achieves a degree of transcendence confronting a beyond. This beyond is experienced as sacred and is responded to with corresponding ambivalence. It is attractive and fascinating, albeit daunting and even threatening.

Some of the men we have considered lead us to believe that the religious response is not the only possible response to the ultimate. They suggest that what is really faced at the limit-situation is a void. Whereas the religious man affirms a "something more," the non-religious man sees simply a "nothing else." Albert Camus gives us a moving description of this "negative religious experience" in his novel, *The Stranger*, wherein a man condemned to die on the morrow achieves a feeling of serenity in the face of an impersonal and indifferent cosmos. This man displays at the limit-situation the same incapacity for relationships that he has exhibited in his daily experiences. Thus his final response at the limit-situation is a projection of his normal response to others.[24]

The reality of what is experienced at the limit-situation, and the answer to the related question: "What is it? 'Something more' or 'nothing else'?", both lie beyond the scope of social science. Yet social science does have something to say with respect to them that has significance and is worthy of attention by theologians and religious thinkers. To follow this matter further, let us consider the contribution of Sigmund Freud to this subject.

Freud presents a striking picture of how the limit-situation impinges upon man in situations of ultimate contingency, powerlessness, and scarcity which we have already described. Nature, says Freud, often shows itself to us in ways that mock our best efforts to control it. The task of culture is to defend us from nature, and from this effort come all the achievements of civilization. Freud distinguishes two aspects of culture: "all the knowledge and power that men have acquired in order to master the forces of nature and win resources from her for the satisfaction of human needs"; and also "all the necessary arrangements whereby men's relations to each other, and in particular the distribution of the attainable riches, may be regulated." [25]

[24] See Albert Camus, *The Stranger*, trans. by Stuart Gilbert (New York: Vintage Books, 1954).

[25] Sigmund Freud, *The Future of an Illusion*, trans. by W. D. Robson-Scott (Garden City, N.Y.: Doubleday, 1957), p. 3.

But these responses to contingency, powerlessness, and scarcity always prove inadequate; they produce results which at best still fall short of men's aspirations, and they very frequently result in frustration and deprivation. Religion, says Freud in an analysis quite similar to that of the functional theorists, compensates for both these grave difficulties. It also aids social control by helping to keep men's anti-social tendencies in line, at least to some tolerable degree. Culture requires "a certain measure of coercion," and men "are not naturally fond of work, and arguments are of no avail against their passions." [26]

Thus far Freud's analysis has coincided with functional theory—but he now advances two new ideas. First of all, religion has done a poor job in defending us against nature, including our own nature. "It is doubtful whether men were in general happier at a time when religious doctrines held unlimited sway than they are now; more moral they certainly were not. They have always understood how to externalize religious precepts, thereby frustrating their intentions. And the priests, who had to enforce religious obedience, met them half way." [27] Second, religion is an illusion, for the significant psychoanalytic reason that "wish-fulfillment is a prominent factor in its motivations," while it disregards the relationship of its content to reality.[28]

Religion, Freud states, "is born of the need to make tolerable the helplessness of man." Freudian analysis has shown not only that human conduct springs from hidden and obscure motives, but that it often re-enacts, in a current situation, behavior learned in and appropriate to earlier situations. These earlier responses are usually of an infantile or "archaic" kind, recapitulated in adulthood in a disguised form. The importance of this Freudian insight is no longer doubted. Religion, for Freud, presented a striking example of this kind of recapitulation. It was a re-enactment of the infantile in the face of the limit-situation.

"For the individual, as for mankind in general, life is hard to endure," says Freud. The human situation is one of "helplessness" and "defenselessness." Thus "man's seriously menaced self-esteem craves for consolation, life and the universe must be rid of their terrors, and incidentally man's curiosity, reinforced, it is true by the strongest practical motives, demands an answer." Religion takes the first step in this direction by humanizing nature, and with this "much is already won." Religion makes for us a world in which, though threatened, we can to some degree "feel at home." "We are perhaps still defenseless, but no longer helplessly paralyzed; we can at least react; perhaps indeed we are not even defenseless, we can have recourse to the same methods against these violent supermen of the beyond that we make use of in our community; we can try to exorcise them, to appease them, to bribe them, and so rob them of part of their power by thus influencing them." But such behavior is not simply contemporary; it contains a substantial recapitulation of the childish past:

[26] *Ibid.*, pp. 7–8.
[27] *Ibid.*, p. 67.
[28] *Ibid.*, p. 54.

the religious experience

For there is nothing new in this situation. It has an infantile prototype, and is really only the continuation of this. For once before one has been in such a state of helplessness: as a little child in one's relationship to one's parents. For one had reason to fear them, especially the father, though at the same time one was sure of his protection against the dangers then known to one. And so it was natural to assimilate and combine the two situations. Here, too, as in dream-life, the wish came into its own.

Thus "man makes the forces of nature not simply in the image of men with whom he can associate as his equals—that would not do justice to the overpowering impression they make on him—but he gives them the characteristics of the father, makes them into gods, thereby following not only an infantile, but also, as I have tried to show, a phylogenetic prototype." [29] Man, at the limit-situation, threatened by the overwhelming character of the confrontation, recapitulates his childhood experience, and religion comes into the world. For Freud, religion is a recapitulation of the infantile, and maturity means putting aside childish things. Freud asserts that despite the assurances and consolations of religion, "man's helplessness remains," and that religious ideas which "should solve for us the riddles of the universe and reconcile us to the troubles of life" are themselves largely unfounded and have "the weakest possible claim to authenticity." [30] Freud takes his position with forthrightness: Man should give up infantile responses and wish-images. Man will then "find himself in a difficult situation. . . . He will have to confess his utter helplessness . . . that he is no longer the center of creation . . . [but] is it not the destiny of childishness to be overcome?" [31]

Freud's treatment of religion raises significant questions for the sociology of religion. Although the ultimate problem of what is actually involved in the religious experience lies beyond the scope of science and is a matter of faith, an analysis of the empirical characteristics of this experience raises fundamental questions. That much religious behavior contains markedly important elements of infantile projection is undoubtedly a justified statement on Freud's part. It is in fact one made by many theologians and religious writers as well. Does not Freud in his treatment unintentionally raise the question of the possibility of mature religion and a mature response that is genuinely religious? Is the "nothing else" response the only mature response at the limit-situation? Is the sacred simply an infantile projection born of experience with the parents? Freud has pointed to the very real basis of infantile elements in religion. It would be hazardous indeed to ignore his contribution. But it would be equally hazardous to dismiss the men from Plato to Otto and Tillich who suggest another possibility. The sociologists of religion must leave these questions open. As a social science, sociology must take a naturalistic approach to the study of religion, but it must also remain sensitive to those areas where men take diverse points of view based upon their commitments of faith.

[29] *Ibid.*, pp. 24–27.
[30] *Ibid.*, p. 45.
[31] *Ibid.*, p. 88.

The Religious View

In the Judeo-Christian religions (as in other world religions) a body of theology has developed possessing significant relevance to the problems we have been discussing. *Theology is the attempt to use the rational philosophical method in explaining what is involved in the religious experiences of various traditions.* In the West, the attempt has been mainly to apply this method to the implications of the Christian experience as understood in the primitive church and as recorded and transmitted in scripture and tradition. According to Christianity, God has revealed himself to men, and thereby the transcendent has broken in upon and become a part of human history. The history of the Hebrews and of the Christian church is from this point of view seen as the unfolding of a dialogue between God and men in which God has called men and has in turn answered their response to his call.

> God, who at sundry times and in diverse manners spake in time past unto the fathers by the prophets,
> Hath in these last days spoken unto us by his Son, whom he hath appointed heir of all things, by whom also he made the worlds. (Hebrews 1:1–2)

According to this view, beginning with Abraham and culminating in Jesus of Nazareth, God has established a relationship with men which is continued in institutionalized Christianity. Such a view is admittedly supraempirical, since "No man has seen God at any time" (I John 4:12). It rests upon faith, which it defines as a divine and supraempirical gift of the Holy Spirit, "the substance of things hoped for, the evidence of things unseen." (Hebrews 11:1)

To the original statement based upon the preaching of Jesus' apostles (the apostolic kerygma), Christian thinkers have added definitions and interpretations using the concepts and insights of Greek philosophy. What does this theology say with respect to the religious experience? Does it say anything of importance to the sociological study of religion?

The main elements of the religious experience as disclosed in our analysis are: the limit-situation; relationship with a beyond, and the supraempirical character of this relationship; the I-Thou content of this relationship, and the sacred character of the beyond; the charismatic character of the experience—its character as call (involving the obligation of response) and its basis in faith and its vulnerability to doubt. All these are seen in the Christian experience and its theological explication. That this theological tradition confirms the main elements found in our own analysis of the religious experience is significant.

What we have done in this chapter is to make indirectly a phenomenological analysis of the religious experience. We have examined the structure of the religious experience as it has impinged upon those who have undergone it. We have done this indirectly by using the works of other

the religious experience

authors in several relevant fields. But we have also seen that religion, while distinct and different from non-religious phenomena, shares important traits with such phenomena. In our day, movements such as nationalism and communism, exhibit in both structure and content many characteristics similar to religious movements.

Joachim Wach, in an important work on the sociology of religion, has suggested four universal criteria by which religious experience can be recognized. First, religion "is a response to what is experienced as ultimate reality; that is, in religious experiences we react not to any single or finite phenomenon, material or otherwise, but to what we realize as undergirding and conditioning all that constitutes our world of experience." Second, religious experience is "a total response of the total being to what is apprehended as ultimate reality. That is, we are involved not exclusively with our mind, our affections or our will, but as integral persons." Third, religious experience "is the most intense experience of which man is capable. That is not to say that all expression of religious experience testifies to this intensity but that, potentially, genuine religious experience is of this nature, as is instanced in conflicts between basic drives and motivations. Religious loyalty, if it is religious loyalty, wins over all other loyalties. The modern term 'existential' designates the profound concern and the utter seriousness of this experience." Fourth, religious experience "involves an imperative, a commitment which impels man to act. This activistic note distinguishes it from aesthetic experience, with which it shares the intensity, and joins it with moral experience. Moral judgment, however, does not necessarily represent a reaction to ultimate reality."

Wach states that unless all four of these are present we are not dealing with genuine religious experience. "However, there are pseudo-religious and semi-religious experiences," says Wach. "The former are non-religious and known by those using the forms to be so. The latter may show the presence of the second, third and fourth characteristics, but not refer to ultimate, but to some aspects of 'finite' reality." [32] The consideration of such "quasi-religious" experiences and the movements and institutions which derive from them offers material of great significance to the sociology of religion. These phenomena affect the position of religion in society, take over some of its functions, and at times enter into serious conflict with religion and religious institutions.

Out of the responses of men to religious experiences, religious groups form and religious institutions develop, religious ideas are elaborated and religious practices are standardized. To this process of institutionalization we must now turn.

[32] Joachim Wach, *Types of Religious Experience, Christian and Non-Christian* (Chicago: University of Chicago Press, 1951), pp. 32–33.

the institutionalization of religion

three

There are two chief kinds of religious organization found in human societies. In primitive and archaic societies, religion is a diffuse phenomenon; many forms of human association, from the family to the work group, have in some important respects a religious character. In these societies, religion is one aspect of the life of all social groups. However, religious and magical specialists appear early in societal development, and religious individualism may be found in contemporary non-literate societies. In time, organizations whose main function is religious make their appearance. These specifically religious organizations are found generally in societies in which an internal differentiation of function and consequent stratification have developed. The appearance of such specifically religious organizations represents one aspect of the increasing division of labor and specificity of function which is an important attribute of urban societies. In traditional societies the same social groups provide satisfaction for both expressive and adaptive needs; in modern societies, organizations which meet adaptive needs tend to be separated out from those which provide an outlet for expressive needs. Tönnies has called the former type of social organization *Gemeinschaft*, the latter *Gesellschaft*. Specifically religious organizations tend to appear as part of the development of *Gesellschaft*.[1]

[1] Ferdinand Tönnies, *Gemeinschaft und Gesellschaft*, trans. by Charles P. Loomis in *Fundamental Concepts of Sociology* (New York: American Book Company, 1940). This

Specifically religious organizations evolve out of the specific religious experiences of particular founders and their disciples. From such experiences a form of religious association emerges, which eventuates in a permanent institutionalized religious organization. The religious experience, as we have seen, marks a breakthrough from the ordinary; it is a charismatic experience. The evolution of stable forms out of this "charismatic moment" is an important example of what Weber called "the routinization of charisma." [2]

Specifically religious organizations are most typical of founded religions which begin with a charismatic figure and a circle of disciples. With the disappearance or death of the charismatic figure himself, a crisis of continuity is created. Weber has shown that if charisma is not "to remain a purely transitory phenomenon, but to take on the character of a permanent relationship forming a stable community of disciples or band of followers," its character must become radically changed.[3] Pure charisma exists only in "the process of originating." The maintenance of the group and the charisma upon which it rests requires a radical alteration of charisma and the authority based upon it. Weber suggests that the motivations for this change are found in the interests, both ideal and material, of the followers, and particularly the leaders among them, to continue the community the founder has created.[4] This means their desire to continue so far as possible under new conditions the original religious experience. This crisis of continuity is also a crisis of succession—who shall constitute the authority in the group to replace the charismatic founder? Weber suggests that the way this crisis is met "is of crucial importance for the character of the subsequent social relationships." [5]

Our analysis of the religious experience in the previous chapter calls our attention to another aspect of the origin and development of founded religions. Our analysis was necessarily an abstract one which attempted to delineate the general outline of the structure of the religious experience; that is, to identify the universal elements of that experience. In the study of a religion, however, it is also important to know the specific content of the religious experience involved, or of what theologians would call the "revelation." For the kinds of stable forms which evolve in the development of religious organization will bear a significant relationship to the content of the religious experience of the founder or founders.

The evolution of founded religions represents a complex social process of which both the routinization of charisma and the continuation in altered form of the original religious experience are important aspects. The foundation of Christianity offers an example. It appears quite clearly in the scriptures that the crucifixion of Jesus was a severe blow to his followers. Upon his arrest, the disciples scattered; Peter alone made his way to the courtyard of the place of trial, only to deny his leader. Again, according to the New

basic dichotomy is treated throughout the sociological literature. See also the works of Robert Redfield, Max Weber, and Talcott Parsons. Parsons' development of the pattern variables is an important contribution in analysis in respect to the two types of society.

[2] Max Weber, *The Theory of Social and Economic Organization*, trans. by A. M. Henderson and Talcott Parsons, Talcott Parsons (ed.) (New York: Oxford University Press, 1947), pp. 363–392.

[3] Weber, *op. cit.*, p. 364.   [4] *Loc. cit.*   [5] *Loc. cit.*

Testament account, the disciples, following Jesus' death, went to Galilee—there, it is said, to await his resurrection (Matthew 28:16). Yet behind this would seem to lie a story of disappointment and defeat. The two who had gone on to Emmaus from Jerusalem, in talking of the terrible recent events in the capital, expressed this feeling: "But we trusted that it had been he which should have redeemed Israel: and besides all this, today is the third day since these things were done." (Luke 24:21). But this pessimism was dispelled by the conviction that Jesus had conquered death, had risen from the dead, and appeared to his followers. In the words of a great Pauline scholar: "It was the Easter experiences of Simon Peter and the others which formed the origin of the Jesus-cult, exceptionally moving religious experiences of exceptional people. . . . These apostolic experiences are the psychological starting-point for the first Jesus-cult in Palestine and the genuine precondition for the rise of the Christian cult-community which now began to organize itself." [6] From this came the belief in Jesus as the "Risen Lord," upon which the early Christian church was founded.

A central concern of this early Christian community was the gatherings which took place daily (Acts 2:46; 5:42), and soon especially on one day, the Lord's Day (I Corinthians 16:2; Acts 20:7), at which a worship service was held. The Book of Acts tells us that religious instruction, preaching, prayer, and the breaking of bread were involved. We know that the first Christians expected a second coming of their Lord in the near future, and that this spirit of expectation infused their meetings. We also know that this breaking of bread was part of the meal which was believed to realize once again Christ's presence, and that in the eating of the bread and the drinking of the wine it was believed that "a direct and intimate union with Christ was achieved" (I Corinthians 11:23 ff). This service reached its climax in "the 'coming of Christ' in the Lord's Supper," [7] since it was believed that "here Christ united himself with his community as crucified and risen and makes it in this way one with himself . . . (I Corinthians 10:17)."

Two things should be noted here. First, the relational nature of the early Christian worship: It maintained a relationship with Jesus as "Risen Christ." Second, the new body of believers, while it does other things, such as preaching and aiding its members, and although its members still participate in the rituals of the Jewish Temple, is centered upon worship—upon cultic activity. Here we see the central importance of the continuation of the religious experience. In this description of the early church, we see the three levels or three aspects which make up the process of institutionalization. Religious institutions evolve as patterns of worship—that is, as cult; they evolve at the same time as patterns of ideas and definitions—that is, as beliefs; and they emerge as forms of association or organization. Religious

[6] Adolf Deismann, *Paul: A Study in Social and Religious History*, trans. by William E. Wilson (New York: Harper, 1957), pp. 122–123.

[7] These two quotations are from Morton Scott Enslin, *Christian Beginnings*, Parts I and II (New York: Harper, 1956), p. 17; and Oscar Cullman, *Early Christian Worship*, trans. by A. Stewart Todd and James B. Torrance (London: SCM Press, 1953), p. 26. The presentation in this chapter is indebted to the systematic discussion of this topic in Joachim Wach, *Sociology of Religion* (Chicago: University of Chicago Press, 1944).

the institutionalization of religion

institutionalization occurs on the intellectual level, the cultic level, and the organization level. These are three sides or aspects of one developmental process. Here in the Christian case we see these three aspects as part of a whole. In the preaching we have the statement of what is believed, its first assertion in discourse. In the cultic activity we see the expression of basic attitudes in the relationship to sacred things—the re-enactment of the relationship to Jesus as Lord. In the brotherhood of believers we have the first form of organization. From the preaching developed creeds and theology; from the cult, elaborate symbolic liturgies; from the brotherhood, the ecclesiastical organization.

Although the Christian church is but one example, which like all others has its particular characteristics and circumstances, it offers a striking model for the continuation of the religious experience and the relationships based upon it—the transformation of charisma into stable forms of thought, practice, and organization. Let us now turn, without confining ourselves to the Christian example, to the institutionalization of religion on the three levels we have discussed.

The Cult

That complex of gesture, word, and symbolic vehicle which is the central religious phenomenon we call the *cult*, is first of all an *acting out* of feelings, attitudes, and relationships. The feelings, attitudes, and relationships so acted out have, as Malinowski pointed out, no other end than themselves. They are acts of expression. "The cult has a mysterious value which is attached to it that we cannot fully rationalize." [8] The relationships acted out in the cult are first of all relationships with the sacred object, however the particular religion conceives it. They are only secondarily relationships among the members and between members and leaders, relationships implicit in the cultic act itself. In the history of Christianity there is no evidence that the Eucharistic meal was such that the leading role in it could be taken by anyone. It is here that we find one of the important roots of the division that develops later between clergy and laity. Since the religious experience is not simply a philosophical or intellectual experience but involves the feelings and acts of men, so the cultic act which continues it is not simply a matter of assertions of faith. It is a "rich and complex action in which his [the worshipper's] whole nature is concerned, and which has at its full development the characters of a work of art." [9] Such religious ritual, which consists of speech, gesture, song, sacramental meals, and sacrifice "is not prescribed for a practical purpose, not even that of social solidarity. Such solidarity may be one of its effects . . . but neither myth nor ritual arose originally for this purpose." [10]

[8] George Herbert Mead, *Mind, Self and Society*, Charles W. Morris (ed.) (Chicago: University of Chicago Press, 1934), p. 296.
[9] Evelyn Underhill, *Worship* (New York: Harper Torchbooks, 1957), p. 23.
[10] Susanne K. Langer, *Philosophy in a New Key* (Cambridge, Mass.: Harvard University Press, copyright 1957 by the President and Fellows of Harvard College), p. 48.

39

Ritual is a symbolic transformation of experiences that no other medium can adequately express. Because it springs from a primary human need, it is a spontaneous activity—that is to say, it arises without intention, without adaptation to a conscious purpose; its growth is undesigned, its pattern purely natural, however intricate it may be.[11]

Ritual and liturgy as the acting out of attitudes develop also around the important incidents, crises, and transitions in the life of the individual and the group. Birth, puberty, marriage, illness, changes of status, and death are marked by sacramental ritual in all religions. In non-literate and archaic societies, in which religion is a more pervasive phenomenon than it is in modern societies, such rites are omnipresent. These *rites of passage*, practiced universally, "consecrate the crises and marginal situations in individual and collective life." [12] In such crises men are potentially exposed to the dangers involved in the contingency and powerlessness inherent in the human condition. All these rites express what we have called, following Martin Buber, an I-Thou attitude toward the sacred.

The cult begins as spontaneous expression, although, as in the early Christian case where much was borrowed from the synagogue, traditional materials may be utilized. But as time goes on, both elaboration and standardization occur, and set rubrics are established. "Proper" (traditional) performance becomes an important consideration. By the time Justin wrote his *Apology* in 150 A.D., in which he described the Eucharistic service of the Christian church, free expression of emotion characteristic of earlier meetings, such as "prophesyings, speaking with tongues and interpretation of tongues," had disappeared.[13] In the Christian church several liturgies in several languages evolved, all similar in their basic ritual and symbolic content, and it became possible to speak of the church as divided into liturgical provinces. In this process of standardization, the rites of worship—the Mass or Liturgy —were gradually established.[14] The cult became both the re-presentation of the original experience *and* the way in which the worshippers expressed their relationship to the sacred.

The institutionalization of ritual, the patterning of its words, gestures, and procedures, means a kind of sharing and objectification of the originally subjective and spontaneous attitudes of the believers. Such a sharing and objectification is necessary in order to preserve under the new conditions of developing institutionalization the original expressive activity. The result of this sharing and objectification is established ritual, which now *elicits* attitudes instead of directly *expressing* them. Ritual represents "the formalization of behavior in the presence of the sacred objects."

---

[11] *Ibid.*, p. 40.
[12] Joachim Wach, *Types of Religious Experience, Christian and Non-Christian* (Chicago: University of Chicago Press, 1952), p. 42.
[13] Cullman, *op. cit.*, p. 30.
[14] L. Duchesne, *Christian Worship: Its Origin and Evolution*, trans. by M. L. McClure (New York: Gorham, 1904).

the institutionalization of religion

Ritual "expresses feelings" in the logical rather than the psychological sense. It may have what Aristotle called "cathartic" value, but that is not its characteristic; it is primarily an *articulation* of feelings. The ultimate product of such an articulation is not a simple emotion, but a complex, permanent *attitude*.[15]

The rite is a "constant reiteration of sentiments" and a "disciplined rehearsal of 'right attitudes.' " [16] But the rite does have great functional significance for the group, despite the fact that this is not the intention of its participants. The cultic act in its "reiteration of sentiments" and its "rehearsal of right attitudes" acts out and reinforces the solidarity of the group. Parsons has said: "For by the common ritual expression of their attitudes men not only manifest them but they, in turn, reinforce the attitudes. Ritual brings the attitudes into a heightened state of self-consciousness which greatly strengthens them, and through them strengthens, in turn, the moral community." [17] Thus the cultic act is a social or congregational act in which the group re-enacts its relationship to the sacred objects and, through them, to the beyond, and in so doing reinforces its own solidarity and reaffirms its own values. In it, relationships of fellowship, and of leader and followers, are acted out, reasserted, and strengthened. For the individual, it incorporates him into the group which provides him with emotional support, and by its re-enactment of the religious experience relates him to the source of strength and comfort.

The Emergence of Belief Patterns (Myth)

The second level or aspect involved in the institutionalization of religion is the level of beliefs or the intellectual level. We may divide the intellectual expression of religion into two major modes, the *mythic* and the *rational*. Myth is the primordial form of the intellectual expression of religious beliefs and attitudes. It has been said that myth "is primitive philosophy, the simplest presentational form of thought, a series of attempts to understand the world, to explain life and death, fate and nature, gods and cults." [18] But myth is also a complex kind of human assertion. It is a dramatic assertion, not simply a rational statement. It is a dramatic assertion in which the thoughts and feelings, attitudes and sentiments, are involved. Levy-Bruhl, who correctly recognized the element of mystic participation by both the teller and the listeners in mythic communication, unfortunately conceptualized his insights in terms of logical and pre-logical forms of thought. This distinction did not prove helpful to understanding the meaning of myth. Ernst Cassirer, the great student of

[15] Langer, *op. cit.*, p. 153.
[16] *Loc. cit.*
[17] Talcott Parsons, *The Structure of Social Action* (Glencoe, Ill.: The Free Press, 1949), p. 435.
[18] E. Bethe, *Mythus-Sage-Märchen* (Leipzig, 1905). Quoted from Langer, *op. cit.*, p. 144.

symbolism, pointed out that what is characteristic of the primitive mentality "is not its logic but its general sentiment of life." Primitive man looks at nature with a degree of participation in its events and processes. "His view of nature is neither merely theoretical nor merely practical; it is *sympathetic*. If we miss this point we cannot find the approach to the mythical world . . ." [19] Cassirer goes on to say:

> Myth is an offspring of emotion and its emotional background imbues all its productions with its own specific color. Primitive man by no means lacks the ability to grasp the empirical differences of things. But in his conception of nature and life all these differences are obliterated by a stronger feeling: the deep conviction of a fundamental and indelible solidarity of life that bridges over the multiplicity and variety of single forms. . . . The consanguinity of all forms of life seems to be a general presupposition of mythical thought.[20]

Cassirer also points out that myth perceives and presents a world that is "fluid and fluctuating" unlike the theoretical world of traditional philosophy. Moreover, he states:

> The world of myth is a dramatic world—a world of actions, of forces, of conflicting powers. . . . Whatever is seen or felt is surrounded by a special atmosphere—an atmosphere of joy or grief, of anguish, of excitement, of exultation or depression. Here we cannot speak of "things" as dead or indifferent stuff. All objects are benignant, friendly or inimical, familiar or uncanny, alluring and fascinating or repellent and threatening.[21]

Through myth, men not only "explain" their world but symbolically re-present it. Myth involves another way of seeing the world, a way which expresses its coherence together with human emotional involvement and participation in it. Myths are serious expressions of a relation to the world. "In myth and by means of the mythic image, there is an externalization of the inner stirring, the emotion of man as he meets the world, his receptivity to impulses coming from the 'outside,' the communality of substance which welds him to the totality of beings." [22]

In myth, man asserts his apprehension of what the Stoics called "the sympathy of the whole," and of his part and participation in that whole. Myth is the emotion-laden assertion of man's place in a world that is meaningful to him, and of his solidarity with it. Such a spontaneous and non-rational assertion, dramatically put forth, is a response to some degree of recognition that there is a separation of man, with his human consciousness, from the whole, and also a felt need to reassert and thereby re-form the connection.

The mythic stands outside—beyond—both time and the empirical world.

[19] Ernst Cassirer, *An Essay on Man* (Garden City, N. Y.: Doubleday Anchor Books, 1953), p. 109.
[20] *Loc. cit.*
[21] *Ibid.*, pp. 102–103.
[22] Eric Dardel, "The Mythic," *Diogenes* (Summer 1954), 7:35–36.

the institutionalization of religion

Mythic time is always present, and myth re-creates and re-presents what it portrays; it actualizes what it tells. Standing outside of time, making present what it presents, myth tells the event itself, not a mere description of it. It makes past and future immediately present; it expresses man's solidarity with his world, and reasserts that solidarity in the face of human doubt. "If the mythic is the language of a man who feels himself thoroughly at one with the world, part of the world, form amid the forms of the universe, it is also the first rupture in his being, the first flight above, which makes the real unreal, and detaches man from his environment, and so a source of all poetry and all culture." [23] Myth is "not reflective contemplation, but actuality. *It is the reiterated presentation of some event replete with power. . . ."* [24] It is a celebration of a primordial reality rendered actively present to which the teller and listener are related by emotional participation. Through it men are related to their environment, to their ancestors, to their descendants, to the beyond which is the ground of all existence, to what is permanent beyond all flux.

The Rationalization of Belief Patterns

Besides myth, other ways of apprehension, other thought forms, other modes of explanation develop in human experience. Such developments are often related to culture contact between hetero- geneous peoples, and to inner differentiation of societies into strata with diverse life styles and life experiences. Scholars and thinkers have variously categorized these developments. Auguste Comte spoke of a "Law of Three Stages" involving a *religious* stage, a *metaphysical* stage, and a *positive* stage. By a religious (or theological) stage, Comte understood a period of mythic thought and apprehension; by a metaphysical stage, a period in which objec- tive rational but abstract categories and concepts are used to organize the world of experience; by a positive stage, a period in which the modern scientific mode of apprehension and concept formation are developed. Before Comte, Vico spoke of three ages: (1) an age of *gods*, similar to the mythic period; (2) an age of *heroes*, in which men held up to themselves grand models such as Achilles, to give them the courage to project and partially achieve their aspirations of self-fulfillment; and (3) an age of *men*, in which a sober grasp of history would be achieved by men audacious enough to look at human reality without the aids and comforts of myth and epic. Such categorizations of historic transformations of human consciousness suffer from a degree of over-simplification, but they should not simply be dismissed. That some such development of thought forms has occurred is clear enough. But neither should one postulate neat laws of progression, nor overlook the fact that the "stages" often overlap, and indeed are frequently found together in human experience.

Here we shall note what Weber, following Kant's *Essay on Universal*

---

[23] *Ibid.*, p. 36.
[24] G. Van der Leeuw, *Religion in Essence and Manifestation*, Vol. II, trans. by J. E. Turner (New York: Harper Torchbooks, 1963), p. 413.

History, called "the process of rationalization." Human thought has become progressively rationalized, both in a formal sense, with respect to its consistency and its systematic character, and substantively, in the elimination of fantasy and mythic elements. The aspect of this process that is of concern to us is the development of rational theologies. This development has been particularly observable in Western civilization, where the Fathers of the Christian church utilized the concepts and methods of Greek philosophy to explain and spell out the implications of the "deposit of faith" believed to have been revealed in the Bible and the *kerygma* of the apostles.

The development of rational theologies is related to inner changes in the religious organization, in which a professional priestly stratum is progressively differentiated from the rank-and-file members. Although myth is not impermeable to logic, and mythic views become rationalized, this progress from *mythos* to *logos* usually waits upon the development of a priestly group. "The full development of both a metaphysical rationalization and a religious ethic requires an independent and professionally trained priesthood, permanently occupied with the cult and with the practical problems involved in the cure of souls." [25]

Weber pointed out that both in classical China and in ancient Buddhism there developed in the absence of a professional priesthood "something quite different from a metaphysically rationalized religion." [26] And in classical antiquity, where there developed no priesthood of genuinely independent status, "rationalization of religious life was fragmentary or entirely missing. . . ." [27] An interesting contemporary example of this can be seen in American Mormonism, which has no professional clergy and where rationalization of belief has lagged despite genuine theological problems within the content of Mormon belief.[28] In early Christianity, however, a professional clergy and a body of rational theology both arose.

Ernst Troeltsch, in his monumental study of the adjustment of Christianity to the world, pointed out that in the intellectual sphere there took place in the early church a far reaching but selective fusion of the church and classical culture. "Christian writers, scholars, and teachers only appropriated for their own use those elements in the religious and ethical philosophy of late antiquity which had an affinity with Christianity and a similar outlook on the world." [29] "Natural science was ignored" and "history and criticism were left out of account." [30] "In this opposition to the empirical exact sciences Christianity joined forces with the specific tendency of declining antiquity and helped to hasten the decline of critical and purely positive

[25] Max Weber, *The Sociology of Religion*, trans. by Ephraim Fischoff (Boston: Beacon Press, 1963), p. 30.

[26] *Loc. cit.*

[27] *Loc. cit.*

[28] Thomas F. O'Dea, *The Mormons* (Chicago: University of Chicago Press, 1957), pp. 229–230, 234.

[29] Ernst Troeltsch, *The Social Teaching of the Christian Churches*, Vol. I, trans. by Olive Wyon (New York: Macmillan, 1931), p. 142.

[30] *Ibid.*, p. 143.

the institutionalization of religion

knowledge." [31] Yet there did occur a significant acceptance of rationality which was to have far-reaching effects upon both medieval civilization and modern times.

This acceptance of much of classical culture and its rational thought was part of the church's response to its cultural milieu and the threat of "acute Hellenization" which this milieu represented. Some within the church feared and fought this tendency toward acceptance; others advocated it, however, on a selective basis. The German theologian Bultmann has shown that Paul used the vocabulary and conceptions of the Greek Gnostics—which, however, he reinterpreted in a Christian sense.[32] From this fusion of the intellectual heritage of antiquity and the viewpoint of the early church, rational Christian theology was born. The preaching of the apostles and the text of the New Testament, which the early church selected and approved, was integrated with Platonism and with elements of Stoicism in a process which was "so significant for world history," and which produced a rich rational metaphysics.[33]

Rational theology develops as part of the rationalization of thought and is to be found in one form or another in all the world religions. It reflects the preoccupation of strata of religious specialists who make explicit and consistent the intellectual and existential implications of a body of religious tradition. The development of a rational theology also involves the working out of a rational ethic (or moral theology) based upon the practical implications of tradition and the religious experience upon which it rests. The definitions of existence and ethics—of "what *is*" and "what *ought* to be done"—worked out in the evolution of a theological tradition become the taught doctrine of religious organizations. As such, they are brought to bear on the education of the membership. In this way they enter into men's definition of the situations in which they act, their conception of proper goals and the means to achieve them, and thus become "bound up with practical attitudes towards the most varied aspects of daily life." [34]

In his study of the Protestant Ethic, Weber has shown how theological conceptions become part of the deeper felt orientations of human beings and as such affect society and human action in significant ways. Weber saw that trend in Protestantism which tended toward asceticism as having far-reaching effects in the elimination of magical and mythic elements from its religious outlook and correspondingly focusing men's attention and energies on action in the world. He contrasted such an "elimination of magic and the supernatural quest for salvation, of which the highest form was intellectualist, contemplative illumination," in ascetic Protestantism with the condition in the "popular religions of Asia" for whom "the world remained a great en-

[31] *Ibid.*, p. 144.
[32] Rudolf Bultmann, *Primitive Christianity* (New York: Meridian Books, 1956), pp. 196 ff.
[33] Troeltsch, *op. cit.*, pp. 142–143.
[34] Talcott Parsons, *Essays in Sociological Theory* (Glencoe, Ill.: The Free Press, 1958), p. 209.

45

chanted garden" in which one could seek salvation only "through ritualistic, idolatrous, or sacramental procedures." He saw Protestantism alone as creating "the religious motivation for seeking salvation primarily through immersion in one's worldly vocation." [35]

The development of such rational theologies is a part of the shift in thought from *mythos* to *logos*, from the mythopoeic to the rational. Ascetic Protestantism represents the furthest development of this process within the thought-forms of Christianity itself. It completes the great historic process of rationalization of religious thought which began with the early Hebrews. Various cultures and various social strata have contributed to this rationalization process. It involves what Burckhardt called "the disenchantment of the world." It is a process which may be said to go through three phases. In primitive and archaic religions, myth embodies the dramatic I-Thou relationship between men and the sacred aspects of their world. In Biblical religion, Yahweh as the transcendent God becomes the object of this I-Thou relation, and the world becomes his creation. Toward God, one takes an I-Thou attitude; toward the world, an I-It attitude. "The dominant tenet of Hebrew thought is the absolute transcendence of God. Yahweh is not in nature. Neither earth nor sun nor heaven is divine; even the most potent natural phenomena are but reflections of God's greatness." [36] Moreover, this insight of Hebraic religion gives rise to prophetic protest. The social order derives from God but it is not necessarily sanctified and protest becomes possible. Hebrew religion cuts through the "enchanted garden" and moves men nearer to ultimacy—to a more lucid grasp of the limit-situation.

In Christianity, while the Hebrew insights were maintained, the Catholic cultus and the sacramental aids to man's relation to God represented a partial re-sanctification of nature. The middle classes of the Reformation period who embraced ascetic Protestantism found these forms unsuited to their own inner religious needs and broke through them under Biblical inspiration. Emphasizing man's aloneness before God, whose relationship to man was in part conceived of in a manipulative way, with God manipulating man (who actively worked out the implication of his own election), ascetic Protestantism saw the world as an arena for man's active mastery. This prepared the way for the third phase—that of the secularization of culture, and disbelief in the transcendent God. The world became an *it* and as such, man's total setting.

This final development of secularization has another important historic source. Greek culture also experienced a considerable development of rationality. In fact, early Ionian thought "ignored with astonishing boldness the prescriptive sanctions of religious representations." [37] Greek urban man early formulated a new kind of relationship to the world of his experience, an intellectual relationship from which subjective projections and emotional

[35] Weber, *op. cit.*, pp. 269–270.
[36] Henri Frankfort, Mrs. Henri Frankfort, John A. Wilson, and Thorkild Jacobsen, *Before Philosophy* (Harmondsworth, Middlesex: Penguin Books, 1949), p. 241.
[37] Francis Cornford, *Cambridge Ancient History*, Vol. IV, p. 532. Quoted from Frankfort, *et al.*, *op. cit.*, p. 253.

46

participation were increasingly withdrawn. Man's attitude toward his world changed; "from being active and emotional, [it] has become intellectual and speculative." [38] Thus arose the Greek rationality which early Christianity confronted and, after hesitation, adapted selectively to its purposes. Out of this combination arose the philosophy of the Christian Middle Ages. When in the late Middle Ages and the early Renaissance the lay town became a center of cultural influence, a new secularization began.

Biblical religion calls our attention to a second important distinction characteristic of religious beliefs and theologies. Not only is there the distinction between myth and rational theology, but there is also a distinction between immanentist and transcendentalist theologies. *Immanentist* religions see God or the "sacred" as beyond appearances but at the same time permeating the world. Hinduism, Buddhism, Taoism, and many of the religions of non-literate peoples conceive of the divine in this manner. For developed immanentist theologies, experience in the world is in some way "illusion." Even human individuality is seen as but one more empirical limitation enforcing an illusory condition of human consciousness and preventing man from making contact with the immanent divine behind the appearances of the things of the world.

Western theology, on the other hand, presents a more radical rupture with the world of myth. According to this theology, God is transcendent and the world is a thing to be known, handled, manipulated and controlled. Individuation is not merely limitation and real experience is not an illusion. The world and human history are real and to be taken seriously. Christianity used Greek concepts to portray Jesus not only as the Christ, but as the divine *Logos*, the divine reason existent as a person. Western religious thought is *transcendentalist*, with its emphasis upon a transcendent God and upon the world as his creation.

The Emergence of Religious Organization

In primitive societies, religion is broadly diffused among the numerous activities and social relationships of the society. Two factors tend to promote a change from the primitive and archaic situation of diffuse religion and the identity of religious and other social groups to specifically religious organizations. First, there is the increasing inner differentiation of the total society. As its division of labor becomes more proliferated and consequently its allocation of functions, facilities and rewards becomes more complex, a society tends to develop a high degree of specificity of function. Groups based upon a specific purpose come into existence and perform many tasks, productive, educational, and the like, which formerly were taken care of in more diffuse groups such as the family. Specifically religious organizations tend to arise as part of this general tendency toward functional specificity. Second, there is an enriching of religious experience which eventuates in the foundation of new religious

[38] Francis Cornford, *From Religion to Philosophy* (New York: Harper, 1957), pp. ix–x.

47

organizations of various kinds.[39] Thus the development of specifically religious organization represents both the effect of general societal processes and changes in the religious consciousness, the second often not unrelated to the first.

A. D. Nock, in his well known study of conversion in classical antiquity, has pointed out that these new religious groups are often at odds with the established society, its norms and institutions.[40] These new organizations offer a new community and a new pattern of life to their members. They represent a break with the past. This is to be seen in the radical terms of the New Testament: "If any man come to me, and hate not his father, and mother, and wife, and children, and brethren, and sisters, yea, and his own life also, he cannot be my disciple" (Luke 14:26). And Paul also speaks of the new solidarity of the Christian communion which obliterates the distinctions of the past and of the outside world: "There is neither Jew nor Greek, there is neither bond nor free, there is neither male nor female: for ye are all one in Christ Jesus" (Galatians 3:28).

The newly founded religious group will differ from other groups in the society by virtue of its rituals, its beliefs, and its type of organization. It will generally display a break with the past and a new spirit of coherence and unity.[41] Differences, social and ethnic, of the old world and the pre-conversion life are left behind and often explicitly repudiated. While there is often a high degree of fraternal equality, new differences based upon position and function within the new group emerge and are often explicitly recognized and approved.[42] Together with new statuses and functions, the older statuses in the world are often tolerated and recognized, while being explicitly denied. Thus, while in the early Pauline churches there was "neither bond nor free," Paul also counseled that slaves should obey their masters (Titus 2:9).

The problem of how to regard the differences of the established society is part of the more general problem of how the new group will handle its relationship to the established order. Three possibilities present themselves. The first is to reject these older forms of social relations in spirit and in fact. This is a course which gives the new group an active revolutionary character. The second is to make a frank recognition and acceptance of them. Third, it is possible to reject them in spirit, to promote attitudes of equality within the religious organization, while leaving the established forms of social domination and social distance undisturbed. The first possibility is a dangerous path, placing the group in opposition to the status quo. It is often seen by new religious groups as unnecessary, unimportant and superfluous, in terms of an other-worldly orientation. The second possibility contradicts the new spirit of breaking with the past on the part of the converts, and the new solidarity of the religious communion. The third, which was the course taken by the early Christian church, expresses the new character of the group, while permitting it to avoid active opposition to established

[39] Wach, *The Sociology of Religion*, p. 109.
[40] A. D. Nock, *Conversion* (London: Oxford University Press, 1961).
[41] Wach, *op. cit.*, p. 110.
[42] *Ibid.*, p. 111.

48

the institutionalization of religion

society. This third position as taken by the Christian church became a source of egalitarian ideas and values throughout Christian history and was a factor in the rise of secular egalitarianism. But it also expressed the beginning of an accommodation to things as they are, and was an important source of social conservatism in Christian thought. Throughout Christian history these two tendencies, the utopian and the conservative, remain in conflict.

An important aspect of this problem of accommodation, of fitting into the established society while remaining apart from it, concerns the attitude of the new group toward the political authorities. It is an interesting fact that the Christian church, while often persecuted (and at times bitterly) in its early history, never denied the legitimacy before God of the established governmental institutions of the Roman Empire. Here too we see the early appearance of an ambivalence and ambiguity in the Christian attitude which will continue in varied forms under changing historical conditions down through the centuries. The new body asserts its own superiority over the established authorities, but in a way that does not challenge their effective operation or legitimacy. While becoming a community unto itself, the church at the same time recognized and came to terms with the legitimate political authority. Peter is reported in Acts as declaring: "We ought to obey God rather than men" (Acts 5:29). But Paul, in the Epistle to the Romans, states that "the powers that be are ordained of God" (Romans 13:1). The radical implications of the new religious organization are confined to other-worldly implications, and accommodation to and recognition of "earthly authority" are justified and made legitimate.

Moreover, alongside this accommodation to the social order, and to some degree accepting its status differences, there is a process of differentiation that occurs within the religious group itself. From the beginning there are followers and leaders. What the earliest Christian churches looked like in terms of inner organization has been a matter of both research and controversy. Such controversy has tended to reflect partisan division. Protestant historians such as Hase and Harnack tended to present the early church as a relatively undifferentiated community living under a charismatic leadership. Such a view fitted in well with Protestant values and Protestant attitudes toward the Church of Rome. Catholic historians such as Battifol have stressed the importance of authority, first in the apostles and later in the bishops. Such a view accords with the claims of the Catholic position as to the origin and legitimacy of established ecclesiastical authority. In our day the two views have come closer together, and research has been less partisan.

We have seen that charismatic authority is inherently unstable and that its transformation into institutionalized leadership is necessary for the survival of the group. The survival of the Christian church, and its evolved leadership and authority structure by the end of the second century, suggest that such development must possess some degree of continuity with the inner structure of the earliest community. Indeed, in the New Testament we find evidences of those bases upon which such institutionalized authority developed. That Paul speaks with authority seems remarkably clear in the epistles written by and attributed to him. Despite the presence of charismata,

49

preaching by authority is evident: "Therefore, whether it were I or they, so we preach and so ye believed" (I Corinthians 15:11).

Despite the presence of what has been called "mild charismatic anarchy," it appears that the later emphasis upon office and upon received traditions had its origin in the early community. Gradually, out of the division of labor in the cult in which only those specially qualified presided, and in preaching with authenticity, there emerged in the church two distinct status orders: the *clergy* and the *laity*. By the end of the first century, Clement, bishop of Rome, speaks of "high priests," "priests," and "levites," in contrast to "the laity" (Clement XI, 5).

The new Christian group was centered upon worship, on the cult, which in Troeltsch's words "alone made it possible to form a new religious community at all." It was also concerned with preserving its teachings from distortion. In the second century, the contact with Greek thought and the need to preserve the original Christian tradition from corruption gave the emerging ecclesiastical authority a decided intellectual cast. Harnack, the great historian of the development of the Christian dogma, held that it was the challenge of Gnosticism, which sought to give its own shape to a Christianity still relatively shapeless, which "compelled the Church to put its teaching, its worship, and its discipline, into fixed forms and ordinances, and to exclude everyone who would not yield them obedience." [43] Thus the bishops arise not simply as the celebrants of the cult and the channels through which the sacred powers were transmitted to new generations, but also as conservators, defending the core of the Christian faith from misinterpretation. Thus we see that although charisma is a transitory phenomenon which to survive must be incorporated in established forms and offices, these forms as they evolve are themselves threatened by what are considered unauthentic outpourings, and these may indeed be of a charismatic nature. The *routinization* of charisma is therefore a process which also involves the *containment* of charisma.

By the year 200 A.D. the church had assumed a form that would not look unfamiliar to a modern observer. Bishops ruled in the church, holding their office by "apostolic succession"—that is, by tracing the line of their consecration back to the apostles. Doctrine was defined in terms of the apostolic tradition, and more fanciful, if edifying, works were excluded from those read in the worship service and from the New Testament canon. The separation of clergy and laity was established, and the latter entered a condition of tutelage. At the end of the second century, Irenaeus combated the heretics in the name of "that tradition which is derived from the Apostles, and which is safeguarded in the churches through the succession of presbyters," and speaks of the succession of the bishops from the apostles. [44]

Thus institutionalization proceeded on the three interpenetrating levels: *cult, doctrine,* and *organization*. It proceeded out of the need for stability

---

[43] Adolf Harnack, *What Is Christianity?*, trans. by Thomas Bailey Saunders (New York: Harper, 1957), pp. 206–207.

[44] Henry Bettenson (ed.), *Documents of the Christian Church* (New York: Oxford University Press, 1947), p. 96.

50

the institutionalization of religion

and continuity, and the need to preserve the content of religious beliefs. The founding charisma is transformed into the charisma of office, and the relative spontaneity of the earlier period is replaced by institutionalized forms on all three levels. The process of further definition amid inner conflict, often bitter, continues for centuries. The need to answer questions that arise from the implications of the doctrine itself, the need to reinterpret the implications of traditional teachings so as to render them relevant to new situations, and the need to combat extrinsic influences all affect this process.

Five generations after the apostolic age, by the end of the second century, the church in its main structural outlines appeared substantially the same as the Roman Catholic and Eastern Orthodox churches of today. Although bishops and others often displayed heroism and personal charisma in their witness and martyrdom, the church rested upon established office, established cult, and defined doctrine. The cult was the monopoly of the clergy, who ruled and taught and were the institutionalized channel of God's covenanted relations with men. The routinization of charisma had been accomplished and the ecclesiastical organization had emerged. The beginnings of an adjustment to the world had been made, although that process would not reach its full development until after the persecutions of the third century. A rational organization had developed which was capable of further rational legal development. But it was a rational organization which rested upon the re-enactment of its religious experience in the cult, and one strongly committed to its traditional foundations in belief.

What we have called "institutionalization" involving the "routinization of charisma" is a fundamental process in the emergence of religious organization. Equally fundamental and universal is *protest*. Generally all developments, all accommodations to the society, all innovations, give rise to protest from elements within the religious group who are unable to accept the changes. Beginning with the problems involved in containing charisma in the early period, protest appears in one form or another throughout Christian history. Side by side with the institutionalized church of the year 200 A.D. are to be found "numerous 'sects' calling themselves Christian, but denied the name and bitterly opposed." [45] The sects represent protest against the developments in the universal church, now called Catholic, a name first used a century earlier to designate the universal body in contrast to dissenting groups.

Religion and Society

Institutionalization of specifically religious organization is a two-sided process. It involves internal changes in the religious movement and at the same time an adjustment of the religious organization to the general society. The early Christian church, with its other-worldly orientation, faced this problem almost from the beginning. This early church, while rejecting and opposing much in everyday life, accepted the

[45] Harnack, *op. cit.*, p. 192.

world, and did so in two senses. As the inheritor of the Hebrew Bible and of the teaching of Jesus and his disciples, it held against heretical opposition to a creationist theology. God was the world's creator, who had created it through Christ, and the world was in itself good. Christianity long resisted the infiltration of Manichaean doctrines, which preached a radical dualism and saw the world of creation as evil, although such notions dogged Christianity on some semi-conscious level down through the centuries. Christianity accepted the world, but exalted other-worldly values far above it, and thereby denigrated it to a poor second place. In a second sense, the church accepted the world, in its accommodation to and legitimation of the basic social institutions of its time and place. Yet the church also taught that the world was a place of danger for the Christian soul, that it was in some way under the rule of Satan. The community of Christians, while in the world and accommodated to it, was withdrawn and aloof from it.

At any rate, the process of accommodation brought the church into contact with, and placed it in relationship to, the world. In the Roman Empire, which was becoming an increasingly hierarchical society, the clergy became a new class. Although in the first three centuries the clergy supported themselves by means of various occupations, and special clerical dress did not appear until two centuries later, the clergy from Constantine's time were recognized as a special legal class, and later emperors gave them privileges of such nature that the office of bishop became one of highest rank, quite comparable to the status of state dignitaries. Moreover, as time went on, "born Christians," rather than converts, made up the membership of the church, and laxness of observance was not uncommon. The church came to administer large charitable establishments, and became itself the one stable social entity in the faltering empire.

As a result of this process of accommodation, the church was eventually affected by "the world's slow stain." Christians become worldly. Such a development conflicted radically with Christian teachings. While many became affected by the growing worldliness, others tried to live according to the other-worldly teachings, for the church continued to teach suspicion of the world and of worldliness. Riches, ambition, and pleasure were condemned; self-denial and acceptance of suffering were approved. Heroic martyrs provided the model for the Christian witness. *Indifference to* the world, characteristic of the New Testament, became, in the new conditions of accommodation and increasing worldliness, transformed into a *suspicion of* the world. Suspicion of the world included also suspicion of the flesh—a deep anxiety and even fear of sex. Practices of self-denial, and self-inflicted punishments, often excessive, made their appearance.

As part of this reaction, some people in the church voluntarily embraced celibacy and came to live in special groups. Men went into the desert to live a hermit's life, and soon communities which maintained some degree of the hermit's seclusion together with some degree of organization into groups came into existence. Out of these developments *monasticism* arose, consisting of groups of men under a special rule living in isolated little communities. The rise of monasticism represents a *protest* against both the development

the institutionalization of religion

of an institutionalized ecclesiastical body which involved internal routinization, and accommodation to the world, and an *acting out* of an attempt to live according to the teachings of the gospels under the new conditions of the times.

Thus there came into existence a new stratum within the church: neither clergy nor laity, but communities of monks and also of women, claiming a higher ideal—attempting to reinstate the life of the early Christian congregations in the now changed conditions of church and society. The asceticism which characterized this movement turned against the world and the flesh with striking vigor. The body was denied and disciplined; fasting and sexual abstinence were practiced. Monasticism and its extremes of self-denial were at first suspected by the church. It appeared to be a protest movement that by-passed the church's institutionalized means of salvation in the sacraments. In time, more moderate rules were adopted; in the East the rule of St. Basil (329–379) and in the West that of St. Benedict (480–555?) brought both moderation and incorporation of the new movement into the church. Monasticism is a good example of a protest movement which did not eventuate in schism or secession. Instead, it was successfully institutionalized within the church, thereby placing its fervor and energy at the disposal of the church's ideals and aims. Monasteries became centers of liturgical life, emphasizing and developing the cult. The monastic ideal of an ascetic life became the dominant Christian ideal, influencing both the model for clerical and for lay Christian living.

Christianity became in the fourth century the established religion of the Roman Empire, and in the sixth century the church replaced the empire as the one remaining stable social institution in the West. By this time the church was comprised of three social strata. There were the *clergy*, who had defined functions: ruling, teaching, ministering to the members, and celebration of the cult. There were the *monks*, who embodied a way of life characterized by regularized asceticism and living in isolated communities. And there were the *laity*, who remained "in the world," and occupied within the church a position of tutelage.

In time, monks became assimilated to clerics and clerics to monks. Together they made up "the church," which as time went on often clashed with the interests of its "non-religious" members, who happened to be townsmen, feudal lords, princes, or emperors. The church was then for all practical purposes made up of two classes of members: men of religion, and men who lived in the world. By the twelfth century, the great Canonist, Gratian, could write that there were two kinds of Christians: first, clerics and monks; and second, those called lay people. He saw the lay condition as a concession to the weakness of human nature.[46]

We have traced the Christian case of the institutionalization of a specifically religious organization because it offers the best documented example of this process. Other religious movements with different content

[46] See Yves M. J. Congar, O.P., *Lay People in the Church*, trans. by Donald Attwater (Westminster, Maryland: Newman Press, 1957).

in their specific religious experiences and existing in different social and cultural conditions will, of course, follow other paths to routinization. But certain invariant problems illustrated by the Christian case are inherent in the process itself. The establishment of stability, the achievement of continuity, the evolution and formalization of practices and rites, adjustment to the general society and its ideas and values, inner differentiation of the religious group, protest and consequently often conflict and schism—these are universals to be found in the history of specifically religious organizations.

Institutionalization on the three levels, cultic, intellectual, and organizational, is also universal, and, universally, developments on these three levels proceed in intimate interrelationship. In the Christian case we see the central and strategic importance of cult, which continues and re-presents the original religious experience in symbolic transformation. In cultic attitudes and relationships, the germs of both doctrine and organization are implicit. Cult is generally central to developing movements as it is in the early Christian case. Exceptions arise when a religious movement is itself in a fundamental way a protest against cultic developments and practices. In this way ascetic Protestantism became radically anti-cultic and anti-symbolic. These attitudes, however, can only be fully understood in terms of protest against a former condition of the cult itself. Hence the centrality of cult in the development of a religious movement would appear also to be a universal element.

four

Founders of religions, as well as their followers and converts, come from a variety of social groups in societies—from various social classes, strata, and the like. Because these groups have different functions in and receive different rewards from society, they hold different attitudes and different values. The conditions under which they live and their styles of life differ and consequently so do their outlooks, needs, responses, and motivational structures. Some religious ideas will show a marked affinity for the needs and outlooks of some groups, and little or none at all for others. (For example, the Christian idea that Jesus' earthly defeat was in a larger sense a victory over evil and death will be found to have appealed to some classes and strata more than to others.) Consequently, different groups in society will exhibit different kinds of religious needs. As a result, there opens up before the sociology of religion a vast area of study concerning the relation of religion to social structure. There is, however, a two-way relationship here. Not only do social conditions affect the rise and spread of ideas and values, but ideas and values once institutionalized in a society affect the actions of men. Hence the sociology of religion must not only study the effects of social structure upon religion, but also the effects of religion upon social structure.

Moreover, society is not simply a social structure; it is also a complex of social processes. The relationships, values, and goals of society are at any given moment only relatively stable; slow but cumulative changes in them are continually taking place. Other changes are more rapid—so rapid in fact that they cause a visible disruption of the established structure. The breakdown of established social and cultural forms and the emergence of new ones is a process that is continually going on. Obviously, different groups in society are affected differently by social change. Just as some groups perform more significant functions and are more favorably rewarded than are others, so some groups are disposed to oppose change and others to promote it. Some groups have a large *stake*, materially and psychologically, in the going system; others may be indifferent to it and its welfare; while still others may feel strong antagonism to the *status quo* and aspire to see it radically changed.

Clearly, such groups will exhibit different kinds of religious sensitivities. The problem of meaning will differ for groups which live under quite different life conditions. The ways of experiencing the "breaking points" involved in contingency, powerlessness, and scarcity will differ from one group to another. We have seen that men develop their relationship to the beyond after the model of their mundane social relations. As the latter will differ from group to group, so will the former. Moreover, since change involves not only the development of new social and cultural forms, but the breakdown of old ones, some groups are much more affected by the latter than the former aspects of the process. For such groups, exposed to the "structureless" condition of social disorganization and breakdown, the experience of both contingency and powerlessness is often a poignant one.

Durkheim used the term *anomie* to characterize *that state of social disorganization in which established social and cultural forms break down*. He spoke of two aspects of this breakdown. There is loss of *solidarity*; old groups in which individuals find security and response tend to break down. There is also loss of *consensus*; felt agreement (often only semi-conscious) upon values and norms which provided direction and meaning for life tend to break down. While Durkheim saw these as two sides of one process of social disorganization, he showed that the two sides could become disorganized at different rates of speed. The result of the process is a condition of relative isolation and "normlessness" for individuals which Durkheim called *anomie*.[1]

Social patterns emerge because men have need of them, and when such patterns disintegrate, men seek ways out of their predicament—out of the confusion and anxiety which result. Since the experience of anomie is frustrating, men may go over to aggression against real or imagined sources of their difficulties. Moreover, they may try the various means of escape which their situation offers them: pleasure-seeking, alcohol, drugs, or similar things. Finally, they may engage in a "quest for community" [2] and a search for new meaning. From such quests, movements develop which offer new values and new solidarities. Such movements may be religious, or they may

---

[1] For Durkheim's discussion of anomie, see *Suicide*, trans. by John A. Spaulding and George Simpson (Glencoe, Ill.: The Free Press, 1951).

[2] Robert Nisbet, *The Quest for Community* (New York: Oxford University Press, 1953).

56

be quasi-religious, offering less-than-ultimate values and relationships. People suffering from extreme deprivation and people suffering from anomie (some groups may be experiencing both) display a considerable responsiveness to religions which preach a message of salvation—that is, which present the world as a place of toil and suffering, and offer some means of deliverance from it. Christianity is a religion of this kind. It offers the believer salvation through participation in Christ's victory over evil and death. Other social strata with a more positive stake in society and consequently different kinds of religious needs exhibit other sensitivities.

Religion and Social Stratification

Two important conclusions with respect to the relation of religion to social stratification derive from the researches of Max Weber on the world religions. First there is found in the history of these religions—Christianity, Judaism, Islam, Hinduism, Buddhism, Confucianism, and Taoism—a clear and observable relationship between social position and propensity to accept different religious world-views. Second, this is not a hard-and-fast determination of religious outlook by social stratification. For example, the lower middle classes, whom Weber saw as playing a strategic role in the history of Christianity, show "a definite tendency toward congregational religion, toward religion of salvation, and finally toward rational ethical religion." This is in marked contrast to the religious propensities of the peasants. Yet Weber states that it "is far from implying any uniform determinism." Indeed, he says that "within the lower middle classes, and particularly among the artisans, the greatest contrasts have existed side by side," and that the artisans display "a highly checkered diversification." [3]

We shall get a more concrete idea of what is involved in the relation of religion to social stratification if we consider what Weber has to say about the religion of the various classes with which he was concerned. Let us continue with the lower middle classes, especially the urban artisans and small traders. These groups Weber found having far less connection with nature than the farmers and far more involved in a way of life based upon a rational economic foundation. Consequently, their handling of their life situations lent itself to calculability and purposive manipulation. Moreover, he found that honesty was a profitable way of behaving for such groups, and that they tended to believe that work and meeting obligations would bring a "just" reward. "For these reasons, small traders and artisans are disposed to accept a rational world view incorporating an ethic of compensation." [4]

Peasants, in contrast, are involved in the organic processes and the incalculable events of nature. In traditional societies they are not closely integrated into rational market economies. As a consequence, they tend to depend upon magic to influence the irrational and unpredictable cosmic

[3] Max Weber, *The Sociology of Religion*, trans. by Ephraim Fischoff (Boston: Beacon Press, 1963), pp. 95, 96.
[4] *Ibid.*, p. 97.

forces. They are not easily given to ideas of just compensation and are so only when magic has been eliminated—a process in which the artisans are likely to play an important part, not the peasants themselves. Weber states the peasantry as a class will not become the active carrier of a religion unless it is threatened by enslavement or dispossession. While in the early stages of the development of the crafts, the artisan is immersed in magic too, his way of life develops in a rational direction. This is not true of the peasantry unless it is affected by extremely strong outside influences.[5]

Weber found wealthy commercial classes far removed from the belief in the idea of ethical compensation such as appealed to the lower middle classes, and "in all periods of history" possessing a "strongly mundane orientation" which "precludes their having much inclination for prophetic or ethical religion." In fact they are never the "primary carrier of an ethical or salvation religion." The more privileged the position of such classes, the less, according to Weber, are they likely to develop an other-worldly religion.[6]

Warrior nobles live a kind of life which shows very little affinity with the systematic demands of ethics related to a transcendent God, or with ideas like sin, salvation, and humility in any religious sense. The warrior faces death and the irrational and unpredictable elements in human existence as part of his daily life. He is interested in honor and needs from religion protection against evil magic, prayers for victory, or belief in a warrior's heaven. Ethical compensation is not an idea that Weber found developing in the context of the warrior's experience. The adventures and chances of this-worldly existence to a very great extent keep his attention from becoming fixed upon other-worldly aspects of religion.

Weber was much interested in the study of bureaucracy both in Western society and in other world civilizations. He sees the religious tendency of bureaucrats "classically formulated in Confucianism." The result, though aesthetically appealing, is opportunistic and utilitarian. It is a body of conventions displaying "an absolute lack of feeling of a need for salvation or for any transcendent anchorage for ethics." Personal religion of an emotional kind tends to be eliminated. Weber stated that in China the enlightened official kept up the rites for the ancestors and the respect for elders as necessary to the social order, but actually felt a "certain distance from the spirits." [7]

Weber found that the modern industrial working class in Europe showed a predisposition for doctrines of salvation but often of a quasi-religious rather than a religious kind. "In the sphere of proletarian rationalism, religion is generally supplanted by other ideological surrogates." [8] Marx called the European working class a "proletariat." By this he meant to designate a class which had no stake in the ongoing social system. The worker worked and lived in a society of which he was in no genuine sense a part. Marxism became a secular salvation gospel for a large number of the working class between the middle of the nineteenth century and World War II.

[5] *Ibid.*, pp. 80, 97.
[6] *Ibid.*, p. 91.
[7] *Ibid.*, p. 90.
[8] *Ibid.*, p. 101.

religion and society

Weber also spoke generally of the elite and disprivileged classes. Ideas like salvation, sin, and humility Weber found "remote from all elite political classes"[9] and indeed reprehensible to the sense of honor of such classes. He said: "Other things being equal, classes with high social and economic privilege will scarcely be prone to evolve the idea of salvation. Rather, they assign to religion the primary function of legitimizing their own life pattern and situation in the world."[10] Non-privileged and disprivileged classes on the contrary show a tendency to evolve and embrace religions of salvation, "to accept a rational world view incorporating an ethic of compensation,"[11] and to allot a degree of equality to women in religious participation.[12] Weber states: "Since every need for salvation is an expression of some distress, social or economic oppression is an effective source of salvation beliefs, though by no means the exclusive source."[13] On the other hand, Weber concluded that "the classes of the greatest economic disability, such as slaves and free day laborers, have hitherto never been the bearers of a distinctive type of religion."[14]

Situations of social distress have often given rise to messianic movements led by charismatic leaders promising this-worldly or other-worldly salvation to the oppressed.[15] Such movements have been found throughout the world. While in our day such movements tend to be politically oriented and only quasi-religious, most of them in the past have had a definite religious character. Oppressed social strata experiencing the need to be saved from their unhappy situations have evolved utopian ideas concerning divine intervention and the establishment of a kingdom of God on earth. In Judaism such ideas were linked up with the expected coming of the Messiah and the beginning of a messianic age. In Christianity, such ideas have been connected with the second coming of Christ and his reign for a thousand years upon a renewed earth. In other religions, they have taken other forms from sophisticated theological messianism to cargo cults among primitive peoples.[16] Mannheim, the great pioneer in the study of the sociology of knowledge, has shown how out of the perspective of oppressed strata and their longings for deliverance, utopias are born in the minds of men.[17] We saw in the last chapter that the development of specifically religious organizations gave rise to protest movements within such groups. Such manifestations of protest are frequently the result of a combination of both religious and social opposition to developments in both society and religion.

[9] Ibid., p. 85.
[10] Ibid., p. 107.
[11] Ibid., p. 97.
[12] Ibid., p. 104.
[13] Ibid., p. 107.
[14] Ibid., p. 99.
[15] Bernard Barber, "Acculturation and Messianic Movements," American Sociological Review (October 1941), 6: 663–669.
[16] See Vittorio Lanternari, The Religions of the Oppressed, trans. by Lisa Sergio (New York: New American Library, 1965).
[17] Karl Mannheim, Ideology and Utopia (New York: Harcourt, Brace & World, 1949), pp. 190–191.

Weber also pays attention to different religious propensities of women. He found that women display a "great receptivity" to "all religious prophecy except that which is exclusively military in orientation." He also stated that women tended to participate in religious activity with greatly intensified emotional involvement even to the point of what he called hysterical.[18]

What Weber offers the reader are profound insights into tendencies with respect to the relation between social stratification and affinity for religious doctrines. These are not sociological "laws"; they do not claim to state simple and sovereign factors shaping the religious sensitivities of men. Life conditions affect men's religious propensities, and life conditions are significantly correlated with the facts of stratification in all societies. Yet the institutionalization of certain ideas, values, and practices in a society can affect all classes, strata, and groups in that society. When men are socialized in a society and culture, they learn to accept its dominant ideas and values, and this learning is supported by the general opinion of their fellows—by consensual validation. Weber has shown that classes which might never have originated a type of religion can in this way become affected by it. Moreover, certain religious ideas tend to have a universal appeal. Once they are established, for example, salvation religions have a very wide appeal. In the Middle Ages the warrior aristocracy put Christianity and a fighting man's ethic together in the code of chivalry. Weber has said: "Periods of strong prophetic or reformist religious agitation have frequently pulled the nobility in particular into the path of prophetic ethical religion, because this type of religion breaks through all classes and estates, and because the nobility has generally been the first carrier of lay education." [19]

Conversion

In our consideration above of Weber and Durkheim, three things become quite clear. First, inclination toward certain kinds of religious doctrines on the part of people is highly influenced by their social position in society. Secondly, some religious ideas reflect more universal characteristics of the human condition and therefore have a wide appeal which transcends the divisions of social stratification. Thirdly, social change, and especially social disorganization, result in a loss of cultural consensus and group solidarity, and set men upon a "quest for community"—that is, looking for new values to which they might adhere and new groups to which they might belong. This implies that conversion—the acceptance of new religions—is itself closely related to needs and aspirations which are highly affected by the social circumstances of the people involved, although social conditions are not a simple and unique causal element in such cases.

The new doctrines proclaimed by a charismatic leader or by his missionizing followers are in fact a complex mixture of the new and old. Unless they found people's minds in some measure prepared, they would not gather converts. But at the same time they proclaim something new, or something

[18] Weber, *op. cit.*, p. 104.
[19] *Ibid.*, p. 86.

religion and society

old in a new way. In this way they are able to appeal to those who are seeking for new values. A. D. Nock, in his classic study of conversion, states: "The originality of a prophet lies commonly in his ability to fuse into a white heat combustible material which is there, to express and to appear to meet the half-formed prayers of some at least of his contemporaries." [20]

The kind of situation in which conversion takes place may be seen in the early history of the Christian church. Christianity entered the world outside Palestine at a time when the Roman Empire had united a vast area into one political unit and had gone far in breaking down local cultural and ethnic barriers. Urbanization had progressed far—as far, perhaps, as such a development could go before modern industrialism. The breakdown of traditional groups and traditional values was creating a need for a larger world view and a new kind of community in the face of urbanization and its accompanying anomie. Moreover, Christianity came to Europe only after the Roman Empire had established a measure of social and economic stability. The ancient world had gone through several centuries, from the Peloponnesian War to the time of the Gracchi, in which bitter and shattering class struggles were common. Moreover, during this period political ideas of various kinds were widely diffused. But with the rise of the Hellenistic empires in the East and then of Rome, social and economic conditions for large numbers improved. Exploitation and misery for the poor lessened and there was a reduction of the slave markets as a consequence of the *pax Romana*. As a result a middle class rose again. Moreover, there was a decline of this-worldly political ideals, and a marked turn to other-worldly religious and philosophical interests. Troeltsch says: "From the second century, to a great extent, the transcendental interest was paramount, and the desire to improve social conditions in any practical way had died down. . . . The iron stability of the Monarchy influenced the whole spirit of social and political order, and all free movement retired into the sphere of personal, interior life, into the domain of ethical and religious reflection." [21]

Most of the early converts to Christianity came from the lower middle classes of the large cities, who shared in the gradual economic improvement that took place at the time. Yet converts were also made among the very poor, and, as time went on, increasingly among the upper classes as well. Moreover, the largest early conversions were made in the East, where social cleavages were fewer than in the West. Troeltsch states that in general outlook these new communities of Christians were middle class.[22]

Contemporary Conversion

A study of store-front Pentecostal churches among the Puerto Ricans in New York illustrates both the affinity of certain strata for certain religious messages and how membership in a religious organization

[20] A. D. Nock, *Conversion* (London: Oxford University Press, 1961), pp. 9–10.
[21] Ernst Troeltsch, *The Social Teaching of the Christian Churches*, Vol. I, trans. by Olive Wyon (New York: Macmillan, 1931), pp. 40–42.
[22] *Loc. cit.*

offers a way out of anomie. Many migrants found themselves uprooted from old groups, alone, and often mistreated in the new metropolis. The rise of the Pentecostal movement among these immigrants is a typical example of the formation of new religious groups. The study suggests that the formation of these groups represents "a reaction to the anomie involved in migration." [23] It is an example of both the re-formation of solidarity and the development of new values and attitudes. The study details the close and warm solidarity characteristic of the new community of the store-front church and the enthusiasm for the new values espoused by its members. The acceptance of these is experienced by the converts as "regeneration"—a radical break with the past and immersion in a new life. The authors conclude that the formation of these groups is the response to the need for solidarity and the search for new values. It is the "attempt to redevelop the community in the new urban situation." [24] In this conversion too we find that the new ideas and values are not altogether new. Most of the converts were brought up at least nominally as Catholics. Despite the remoteness of institutionalized Catholicism from many of their needs, their background was such as to prepare them to be receptive to the evangelical message of the Pentecostals.[25]

The congruence of the religious message of the Pentecostal movement with the life experience of migrants suffering isolation and disorientation in the metropolis is also evident. The study reports that those interviewed spoke frankly about their conversion. They considered such frank description as a "testimony," a bearing of witness to the work of the Holy Spirit. But the study points out that despite the spontaneity of this witness, there is a degree of stereotyping in the way the conversion is related.

> It would appear that each convert has heard many testimonies and makes the attempt to interpret and fit his own experience into a normatively desired pattern. They usually go this way: "I used to drink . . . I was a drug addict . . . I used to run around with women . . . I was on the wrong path . . . but one day I received the Spirit, I got to know the 'Word'." They always attribute a great sinfulness to their previous life. The form of the testimony emphasizes a great experience of sinfulness and the religious experience of being possessed by the Spirit. And the latter appears to give them a certitude of regeneration.[26]

The study points out that conceptualization in terms of *sinfulness-conversion-regeneration* bears a striking congruity with the actual experience of the converts. The period they see as sinful is that of personal and social disorganization at the time when they were alone and in a genuine sense "lost" in the large city. Conversion means a personal reorganization brought about by identification with the new group and its values. Regeneration describes the state in which as regular members of the new highly solidary

---

[23] Renato Poblete, S. J., and Thomas F. O'Dea, "Anomie and the 'Quest for Community': The Formation of Sects among the Puerto Ricans of New York," *American Catholic Sociological Review* (Spring 1960), No. 1, 21:25–26.

[24] *Ibid.*, p. 29.

[25] *Ibid.*, p. 35.

[26] *Ibid.*, pp. 31–32.

religion and society

and supportive religious group they are sustained in the new values which they now share with their fellow converts.

A. D. Nock, in his study of conversion in the ancient world, has pointed out that Christianity made a much more profound and radical conversion demand than did the other competing religions of the time. One could adhere to the various other groups, but none of them demanded or made possible the full conversion in the Christian and Judaic sense. These religions required a complete turning away from the old and a complete immersion in the new.[27] Only in Greek philosophy, with its idea of a higher life to which it bade men turn, did one find anything really like conversion in the Jewish and Christian sense.[28] Today in New York (and in fact in large cities in Europe and Latin America) such enthusiastic sects bring this message of conversion to men suffering the anxieties and disorientation of anomie. Because their fundamental message, constructed upon the model of *sinfulness-conversion-regeneration*, possesses a strong resonance with the experience of those suffering from anomie and its disorganizing consequences for their lives, these groups are able to convert people and in fact lead them to a new kind of life—to give them the subjective experience of *being saved.*

But we have also seen that in our times religion surrogates perform many of the functions traditionally fulfilled by religion itself. Disprivileged strata under modern circumstances often exhibit a need for salvation and a propensity to accept salvation doctrines, but their specific affinity is for salvation doctrines in non-religious rather than religious form. The socialist movement in the nineteenth and first part of the twentieth century offered to members of the working class who had little or no stake in a developing capitalist society such a salvation doctrine. The socialist movement not only offered new ideas and values but also satisfied a quest for community with its trade union and party organizations. In the present century the growth of communism and nationalism offer a similar spectacle. Such secularized quasi-religious movements offer a kind of belongingness—they satisfy to some degree the quest for community. They also offer an ideological answer to the problem of meaning. Thus to those uprooted and experiencing the anomie and deprivation involved in that condition, secular movements—communism, nationalism, national socialism, etc.—bring the community and sense of worth and meaning formerly associated with religious movements.

Hannah Arendt, in her brilliant work on the origins of totalitarianism, has shown the relation between the quest for community and the search for meaning, and the identification of people with such secular quasi-religious movements. At the core of such phenomena she points to a kind of pseudo-mystical identification with "the movement." The "forces of race" or of "history" become a kind of obscure ultimate that finds its embodiment—its incarnation, to use religious language—in the "party." Similarly, in the new nationalisms, the "nation" offers a similar phenomenon.[29]

[27] Nock, *op. cit.*, p. 114.
[28] *Loc. cit.*
[29] Hannah Arendt, *The Origins of Totalitarianism* (New York: Meridian Books, The World Publishing Company, 1958).

Religion As the Ideology of Transition

In traditional societies, the goals of individuals and groups, and even of society itself, are established and recognized over long periods of time. When, because of contact with other cultures or developments internal to a society, new goals arise and new values come into existence, the leadership of society finds itself in need of an ideology to explain and rationalize the new goals and the values supporting them. Often this process involves the coming to power of new ruling groups. "When elites come to power in periods of crisis, they do so in part by their ability to rally the community around a drive for new goals and by their skill in propounding a new value system acceptable usually to a majority of the community. This system of ideas and aims provides the framework within which the elite organizes a new structure of power and control." [30] In modern times, at least in Europe and America, such new value systems and the ideologies justifying them have been of a secular character.

> The American elite . . . were the direct heirs of the British Whig revolution and the exponents of the value system of Locke and his friends. They laid down in the Declaration of Independence, the Constitution, and the Bill of Rights the rules under which we still operate, rules for protecting "life, liberty and property," to use Locke's phrase, for which Jefferson substituted "life, liberty, and the pursuit of happiness." These are the rules whereby the elite of a national political economy can administer a private enterprise system and a market economy.[31]

Today in the developing nations, national leaders, in order to explain to themselves and to others and to justify the changes they introduce and propose to introduce in their countries, develop statements of interpretation of their histories which set forth goals and render them meaningful. These statements of beliefs and values are ideologies in that "they elicit an emotional commitment by the leadership and their followers and are directed toward action." [32] Thus the ideologies of nationalism and socialism explain and justify the course of transition and the goals involved in it.

In earlier periods of history, religions often fulfilled this function of serving as the *ideology of transition*. In the eighth century, Christianity provided the ideology for the re-establishment of empire for Charlemagne and those about him. Later, in the tenth century, with the establishment of the Holy Roman Empire, it provided the same thing. Perhaps this may be seen most strikingly in the example of the Norse. The conversion of the Nordic peoples to Christianity coincided with the attainment of national unity and a vast process of expansion. Christian kingship, consecrated by ecclesiastical rites and given the sacred charisma of church approval, was an element aiding the development of such unity. Christianity supported and in fact

---

[30] Robert K. Lamb, "Political Elites and the Process of Economic Development," *The Progress of Underdeveloped Areas*, Bert F. Hoselitz (ed.) (Chicago: University of Chicago Press, 1952), p. 34.

[31] *Ibid.*, p. 35.

[32] Paul E. Sigmund, Jr. (ed.), *The Ideologies of the Developing Nations* (New York and London: Frederick A. Praeger, 1963), p. 4.

religion and society

partially inspired these efforts of unification. This can be seen in the lives of men like King Canute in Denmark, and Olaf Trygvason and St. Olaf in Norway. One historian has written: "It was, in fact, only through the authority of a new universal religion that the national monarchy acquired the prestige necessary to overcome the conservativism of the old peasant culture and the independence of the old tribal kingdoms. . . ." [33]

This need of new elites and of peoples in transitions for an ideology is similar to the need of people suffering from anomie for a new value system and a new kind of community. In fact the two needs are often found together. While leaders emerge with a need to develop a definition of their mission in order to know how to act in the situation facing them and in order to legitimate themselves as leaders, followers suffering the anomie of social change search for new values to which they can adhere and new groups to which they can belong. Thus in movements built upon ideologies—whether religious or secular—the leaders find a needed *ideology of transition*, while the followers (and often the leaders too) find satisfaction in their *quest for community* and their *search for new values*.

Conversion and Cultural Prestige

Various groups in their conversion are affected by the cultural prestige which the new religion or ideology carries in their eyes. This may be because of the origin of the ideology, the impressiveness of its content, or its connection with other entities which are highly regarded. For example, in the nineteenth century the claim of an ideology to be "scientific" enhanced its prestige greatly in Europe. Similarly, when Christianity went outside the borders of the Roman Empire, it presented, despite the fall of the empire and the vulgarization of its own ecclesiastical culture, a superior body of knowledge, lore, and belief—the product, even in run-down form, of the high culture of classical antiquity. Moreover, it carried with it the remaining lustre of civilized institutions and imperial dignity. In ways roughly but significantly reminiscent of the propagation of communism in Africa and Asia today, new ideas and new life-orientations were brought to the Celtic and Teutonic peoples of the North.

Religions impress with their charisma—their sacred element—and through its appeal attract followers and converts. This appeal is enhanced by significant elements of cultural prestige. Christianity came to the peoples outside the empire as a fully organized church, a fully formulated dogma, embodied "in a Catholic church into which had passed the conquering and organizing genius of Rome. This finished system was presented to simple peoples, sanctioned by the authority and dowered with the surviving culture of the civilized world. It offered them mightier supernatural aid, nobler knowledge, and a better ordering of life than they had known. The manner and authority of its presentation hastened its acceptance. . . ." [34]

[33] Christopher Dawson, *Religion and the Rise of Western Culture* (Garden City, N. Y.: Doubleday Anchor Books, 1958), p. 95.

[34] H. O. Taylor, *The Mediaeval Mind*, 4th ed. (Cambridge, Mass.: Harvard University Press, 1959), Vol. I, pp. 170–171.

In the conversion of peoples to new doctrines which are products of more complex cultures than their own, the newly accepted ideas often undergo considerable change. Christianity, by the time it came to the North, had worked out its credal statements in terms of Greek philosophical concepts. Marxism, deriving from a re-interpretation of Hegel's philosophy, presents a complicated point of view. Both Christianity and Marxism get vulgarized and oversimplified in their acceptance by people to whom these sophisticated thought systems are unfamiliar in their subtlety or complexity. In addition to being enhanced by extrinsic cultural prestige, such doctrines may be rendered appealing by their gross over-simplification. Indeed, in the case of a religion appealing for converts to people from a more simple culture, magical elements may play as important a part as authentically religious elements. One English historian has pointed out that many among the heathen English "stood in awe" of the Christian missionaries, "fearing their spell-craft." Many were converted because they felt the new religion offered more potent magic. Yet in the same society there were those attracted to the genuinely religious appeal of the new doctrines, especially their other-worldly aspects. "Many Anglo-Saxons were prepared to fix their gaze upon a life to come and to let their fancies fill with visions of the last great severance unto heaven and hell . . . so many a noble thane became an anchorite or a monk, many a noble dame became a nun; and Saxon kings forsook their kingdoms for the cloister. . . ." [35] Yet the cruder magical components were strategically important to the conversion of the North, and their employment led to a vulgarization of religion in the direction of magic among the converted. Speaking of the conversion of what was later northern France, one historian said: "In such a world religion was able to maintain its power only by the awe inspired by its supernatural prestige and the spiritual violence it opposed to the physical violence of barbarism. The fear of the wrath of God and the vengeance of the saints was the only power capable of intimidating the lawless ruffians who were so common among the new ruling class in the semi-barbarous Frankish state." [36]

The Church and the "World"

So far in this chapter, we have considered religion and society in two important respects. We have seen the relationship between religion and social stratification, and we have looked at the kinds of social conditions associated with conversion. *What about the relationships between specifically religious organizations and the societies in which they exist?* The same people belong to specific religious organizations and the other groups of the society. When there is one church and all the people in the society belong to it, as was the case in most Western societies for a long time, how do the church and society affect each other? How do the two actually get along together? The classical study of these questions with respect to Christianity was made by the great German historian and sociologist, Ernst Troeltsch.

[35] *Ibid.*, pp. 181–183.
[36] Dawson, *op. cit.*, p. 33.

religion and society

He summed up such problems in terms of the heading we have used in this section—problems of "The Church and the 'World.'"

Troeltsch points out that the central ideals and values of Christianity "cannot be realized within this world apart from compromise," and therefore the history of Christianity "becomes the story of a constantly renewed search for this compromise, and a fresh opposition to this spirit of compromise."[37] What Troeltsch proposes is that the history of the Christian church is best understood in terms of two contradictory yet complementary tendencies: *compromise with the world* and *rejection of the world*—accommodation, and protest against accommodation.

These constant features of Christian history can be seen in other religious movements and indeed in political movements of a quasi-religious kind involving utopian aspirations. In fact all movements, be they political or religious, which base themselves upon an ideal which ethically transcends the present conditions and is therefore incapable of realization under present conditions without compromise, experience a similar inner conflict. In short, movements, whether secular or religious, based upon a situationally-transcendent ideal, exhibit the conflict between accommodation and protest. In the European socialist movement from 1850 to the present time such tendencies have been evident. The original revolutionary attitudes of the movement became accommodated to the established society, and with the rise of great socialist and Social Democratic parties, piecemeal reform and parliamentary action took the place of the older, more militant forms of opposition. In the foundation of the Third or Communist International, a militant assertion of original doctrines and a strident protest against Social Democratic compromise is to be seen. Again today, with the institutionalization of communism as the official ideology of the established society in the Soviet Union, we see the tendency to compromise and the protest against it. Since the present time is one in which important social conflicts tend to become internationalized, this conflict finds its chief expression in the tension and conflict between Soviet Russia and Communist China, which has infected the other Communist parties throughout the world.

Troeltsch examines the conflict between the ideals and values of Christianity and the institutions of the established society—the conflict between the church and the world in his terms—in four chief areas of Roman society: family life, politics and power, economic life, and learning and thought. In all these areas we see compromise and conflict: marriage is accepted but celibacy is seen as a higher virtue; the established authorities are seen as legitimate but political power is rated low as a value for the Christian; work and even trade are accepted as necessary to society and human well-being, but emphasis upon economic gain is dangerous to the welfare of the Christian soul; and rationality and learning are accepted, but only selectively as they harmonize with Christian beliefs and values.

This conflict and complementarity of compromise and rejection with respect to the general values and institutions of society finds expression in three significant sociological forms. *Compromise* or *accommodation* is em-

[37] Troeltsch, *op. cit.*, Vol. II, pp. 999–1000.

bodied in the *church* which tends to accept, selectively at least, secular culture, and to reconcile itself one way or another with the institutions of the society. The spirit of *rejection of the world and compromise with it* finds organizational expression in the *sect*. Alongside these two basic forms of religious organization, Troeltsch points out a third tendency which has played a most significant part in the history of religion. There is also an individualized response which may come to involve small groups of people. This is *mysticism*. These three types of response to the problem of the church and the world appeared in Christian history from the very beginning.

A considerable amount of research has been conducted in terms of these concepts of Troeltsch, and a number of scholars have developed their theoretical meaning. The definitions of church and sect set forth by Troeltsch and developed by later scholars may be summarized as follows.

The *church* (ecclesia) has the following significant attributes:

1. Membership in fact upon the basis of birth
2. Administration of the formalized means of grace and their sociological and theological concomitants—hierarchy and dogma
3. Inclusiveness of social structure, often coinciding with geographical or ethnic boundaries
4. Orientation toward the conversion of all
5. The tendency to adjust to and compromise with the existing society and its values and institutions

In Troeltsch's words, the church is an "institution which has been endowed with grace and salvation as the result of the work of Redemption; it is able to receive the masses, and to adjust itself to the world. . . ." [38]

The *sect* is characterized by:

1. Separatism from the general society, and withdrawal from or defiance of the world and its institutions and values
2. Exclusiveness both in attitude and in social structure
3. Emphasis upon a conversion experience prior to membership
4. Voluntary joining
5. A spirit of regeneration
6. An attitude of ethical austerity, often of an ascetic nature

In Troeltsch's words the sect is "a voluntary society, composed of strict and definite Christian believers bound to each other by the fact that all have experienced 'the new birth.'" [39]

Troeltsch, Weber, Wach, and others have shown two important "choices" confronting sectarian groups. First of all, like all protest groups, of which they provide an extreme example, they may remain within the general body of the church. In doing so they often become important reforming agencies, and also provide the church with a valuable instrument in its various tasks, charitable and missionary, because of the singlemindedness and fervor of their adherents. Monasticism, as we have seen, was such

[38] *Ibid.*, p. 993.
[39] *Ibid.*, p. 443.

religion and society

a protest movement. It separated itself from the world and displayed many of the sectarian characteristics, but remained within the church an important missionizing and reforming element. The same observation can be made with respect to the mendicant orders of the Middle Ages. Such incorporation is not always done easily. In the case of the Franciscans, for example, it involved conflict with the church, and within the order itself.

The second "choice" or possibility of development for sectarian groups is to secede from the church. The late Middle Ages, the period of the Reformation, as well as later religious history, is replete with examples of such secessionist sects. Secessionist sects are often persecuted by the dominant church, and this atmosphere of persecution enhances the general spirit of sectarian austerity.

H. Richard Niebuhr, Liston Pope, and other students of sectarian development have pointed out that sects also must face the problems raised for their members by having to live within the general society. When children are born to the sectaries, how shall they be treated? Are they to be members? Moreover, ascetic attitudes often lead to hard work and hard work to increasing prosperity. Prosperity tends to make the sectaries conservative; they tend to become better adjusted to the established social order. Niebuhr has noted that if the sect is defined rigorously, it cannot last beyond the founding generation. Family life, increasing wealth and respectability, and routinization, with the passage of time lead to accommodation by the sect. The accommodated and routinized sect has been given the name of *denomination* in sociological literature.[40]

Two other sociologists, Yinger and Wilson, have shown that not all sects are adjusted and routinized in this way. Some of them become *established sects*, which despite changes in their make-up and their situation remain, even with the passing of the founding generation, withdrawn from and/or antagonistic to the general society. Two types of these established sects are to be observed. There are those which literally secede and, finding geographical isolation, build little communities of their own, away from the general society. The Amish, the Hutterites, and others, are examples of this. There are other established sects which remain in the general society—remain in urban areas, in fact—such as the Jehovah's Witnesses and the Christadelphians, but maintain the attitude of opposition to the general society and its values. Such established sects may be said quite paradoxically to institutionalize their opposition to the going society and its culture.[41]

We have already observed that the conflict analyzed by Troeltsch in terms of "the church and the world" is but the Christian expression of a basic conflict characteristic of the experience of all movements which base themselves upon a situationally transcendent ideal. For example, in the communist movement in Europe following World War I, leftist groups objecting to any compromise with the established order arose. Lenin, leader of Russian

40 H. Richard Niebuhr, *The Social Sources of Denominationalism* (New York: Henry Holt & Company, 1929).
41 See Bryan R. Wilson, *Sects and Society* (Berkeley: University of California Press, 1961).

69

Bolshevism and the Third International, condemned this extremely rigid and doctrinaire position as a kind of political sectarianism. He emphasized that even an opposition party of an extreme character had to repudiate any absolute notion of "no compromise."[42] While the socialists considered the communists an extreme "sectarian" group, the communists struggled within their own ranks with those opposing all compromise with the *status quo* even for tactical reasons and branded them "left-sectarians."

Quite clearly, whether in religion or in politics, terms like "compromise" and "rejection" are relative terms. Important religious bodies protested against the Catholic church in the Reformation and set up other churches. These, while largely ecclesiastical in structure, often included some sectarian attributes. In fact, the religious bodies which came into existence in the Reformation varied from *reformed churches* to *independent groups*, which combined characteristics of both church and sect, to groups which were quite clearly *sects*.

A further possibility in the development may be seen in the history of the Mormons. This group, which began with marked sectarian characteristics, did not develop in either of the two directions we have previously discussed. The Mormon church did not become either a denomination or an established sect. The Mormons tried four times in the Middle West to build a city of their own, where had they been successful they might have become a geographically isolated sect. Each time they were driven out, and finally migrated to the West, where they founded their own society. There, in relative isolation, they prospered, attracting many converts from both the United States and Europe. They in fact re-enacted in the sociologically conducive conditions of nineteenth-century America the experience of the biblical Hebrews, whom they sought to emulate. As a consequence they became something resembling an ethnic group—but an ethnic group formed and brought to awareness here in America. They became a "people," to use the term which they quite accurately use to describe themselves. The result is a specifically religious organization as the institutionalized core of a more diffuse social entity with its own history, its own traditions, its conviction of peculiarity, and even its native territory or homeland. What emerged was the Mormon church as the organized core of the Mormon people.[43]

The third response analyzed by Troeltsch is *mysticism*. Mysticism arises when "the world of ideas" which makes up the religious belief system has "hardened into formal worship and doctrine." Religious life then, for some people, becomes "transformed into a purely personal and inward experience." The result is the "formation of groups on a purely personal basis, with no permanent form, which also tends to weaken the significance of worship, doctrine, and the historical element."[44] Mysticism involves the contemplative

[42] V. I. Lenin, *"Left-Wing" Communism: An Infantile Disorder* (New York: International Publishers, 1934).

[43] Thomas F. O'Dea, "Mormonism and the Avoidance of Sectarian Stagnation: A Study of Church, Sect and Incipient Nationality," *American Journal of Sociology* (November 1954), No. 3, 60:285–293.

[44] Troeltsch, *op. cit.*, Vol. II, 993.

70

search for and achievement of the religious experience outside established religious forms. It sees itself as the achievement of a relationship with the beyond, the ultimate, the One—with God—by rising above all forms of the world—both those of the natural and societal environment and those of formalized cult as well.[45] The mystic response is found in all the world religions: in Christianity, Judaism, Hinduism, Buddhism, and even in Islam, where the dominant Sunni point of view is decidedly anti-mystical in its bias. Mysticism is also found in philosophical movements such as Neo-Platonism and the practices of the ancient Pythagoreans. It attracts varied types of people, but especially the intellectual and cultured groups. It does spread to the common people at times, but often in the process it becomes mixed with magical elements—elements which the educated consider superstitious and highly emotional. Leuba, in his study of the psychology of religion, concluded: "If the great Christian mystics could by some miracle be all brought together in the same place, each in his habitual environment, there to live according to his manner, the world would perceive that they constitute one of the most amazing and profound variations of which the human race has yet been witness." [46]

Mysticism is often an expression of protest in a subtle way. While concerned with its quest for a relationship to the divine and not with reform, it expresses a desire to break out of established forms of worship and often of ideas. Like the protest response, however, it can also be reincorporated into the church. Once it becomes incorporated into established religious bodies it contributes considerable enrichment to their subjective religious life. It is not accidental that the fourteenth century saw the development of crisis in the church, the beginnings of scientific and positive thought, and a great increase in mysticism. A European historian gives a vivid picture of this mystical turning inward away from the institutionalized church in the consecration of the great Cathedral at Cologne in 1357:

> Tauler preached a sermon on the theme of the true consecration of churches, explaining that this was a rite to be celebrated within the "inward-turning man." "Churches make no man holy, but men make churches holy." "Holy" Cologne was the largest, richest and most numinous of all the German cities . . . but Tauler and his spiritual brothers found nothing of benefit to man in all this routine and ritual of holiness. The real Empire and the real Church lay within. . . .[47]

Yet mysticism proved to be an important source of vitality both for the older Catholic Church and for the churches of the Reformation.

[45] Evelyn Underhill, *Mysticism* (New York: E. P. Dutton & Company, 1926), p. 96.
[46] Quoted from *Ibid.*, p. 112.
[47] Friedrich Heer, *The Medieval World* (New York: The New American Library, 1963), p. 376.

religion
and conflict
five

The functional theorists emphasize the contribu-
tions made by religion to the continued functioning of society, especially
those which are unintended by the human actors involved. These *latent
positive functions* represent only one kind of effect which religion has upon
societies. Other scholars—historians and social philosophers, for example—
have pointed out that religion can often have a negative effect upon both
the welfare of society and the welfare of individuals. Religious issues have
been among the causes of wars; religious convictions have often given rise to
intolerance and persecution; religious loyalty has united some men only to
divide others. Said Jonathan Swift, who was himself a clergyman of the
Anglican church, "We have just enough religion to make us hate, but not
enough to make us love, one another." We must now pay attention both to
the *ambiguities* of function and the *negative functions* (*dysfunctions*) of religion with respect to societies and individuals.

It will be helpful to recall here some earlier definitions and to propose
some additional ones. By *function* of religion we mean *what religion does for
and to society and individuals*. By *purpose* of religion we mean *what people
intend in their religious behavior*. Functions and purposes may be either
manifest or latent. *Manifest* functions are those *recognized* and *not unintended* by the human actors. *Latent* functions are those *not consciously recognized* and therefore *unintended* by the actors. *Manifest purpose* refers to
what actors *consciously intend; latent purpose* to the *acting out of needs and*

72

motivations which are not fully conscious and fully recognized by the actors.

In Chapter One we saw that religion increases respect for the norms of society by relating them to the sacred. Chapter Three stated, that religious rites renew the respect for the norms, and solidify the coherence of the group. Thus religion has a positive function with respect to social solidarity and social control. But this function is obviously not the intention or purpose of those who believe in the religion and practice the rites. Their manifest purpose is concerned with an answer to the problem of meaning and with acting out in the rites a relationship to ultimacy—to God, the gods, or however the particular religion conceives the sacred object. They may have latent purposes of acting out wishes not fully conscious, but their behavior has positive functions apart from purpose or intention.

When we speak of the function of religion for society, what do we mean by *society*? A society (or social system) is a complex of patterned human behavior exhibiting a high degree of regularity over time. It involves a division of labor, relations of superordination and subordination, differential access to facilities, and differential distribution of both material and non-material rewards. In brief, society involves an allocation of functions, facilities (including power) and rewards. Societies evolve in concrete settings in response to the demands made for human survival, and the satisfaction of human wants, by a given environment. What evolves is a division of labor and of reward: patterned allocation. This patterned allocation becomes legitimated—that is, expressed in norms which the members of society accept as right and proper. There evolves, along with patterned allocation, what Durkheim called *normative consensus.* Such norms then become part of the socialization processes of the society; that is, they are taught to the new generation so that over time as new people replace the old, the same fundamental patterns of expectation and behavior are maintained. These norms are the basis of the patterned or regular behavior and are enforced upon actors by the opinions and reactions of others (*external sanctions*), and by feelings of shame and guilt on the part of the person who breaches or defies the norms (*internal sanctions*). The allocations which evolve are concerned with scarce items: important functions; facilities such as power, property, and position conferring access to things useful and enjoyable; and rewards, whether prestige or material goods. Thus allocation is a process which creates *haves* and *have-nots*; there is *deprivation* involved, both absolute and relative. Consequently, different groups have a different degree of involvement in and identification with the society as it is organized; the various sub-groups in a society each have a different *stake* in the society, its demands and its maintenance. For some groups the stake may be very large, for others it may be minimal, or in fact not exist at all. We have remarked earlier that Marx used the word "proletariat," adapting it from classical Roman usage, to designate the industrial working class of early European capitalism, a class which performed a function but had little or no stake in the society.

Deprivation can elicit active opposition or passive acceptance. The legitimation of norms is one element which by justifying the *status quo* inhibits opposition. It is not sufficient, however. Hence, there develop in every society various social forms which permit tension reduction. These may vary

73

from structured antagonism (permitted but controlled) against internal groups or alien outside groups, to religious rites which allow catharsis of pent-up feelings. Yet despite both the legitimation of norms and the availability of means for tension reduction, every society experiences a struggle or competition of groups attempting to defend or advance their group interests. Such interests are both material and psychological; they involve feelings of worth and dignity as well as access to means for improved living standards. Some groups act to increase their stake in society, and their success often involves important changes in the institutions, and in the relations of sub-groups in the society. Others act in defense of things as they are, since as they are they appear to maximize the interests and stake of such groups. Such social conflict may eventuate in slow but continual reform and reorganization, in abrupt revolutionary change, or in disruption of the society.

One important implication of all this is that societies are stratified; they are composed of different groups—classes, strata, etc.—which perform different functions, possess different degrees of power and influence, have different interests, and receive different kinds and different amounts of reward. We saw earlier that founded religions tend at first to repudiate, at least implicitly, the stratification differences of society, but that after a time they come more or less to accept these social distinctions. Important people in society consequently come to be looked upon as important in the religious group as well. We have also seen that within the specifically religious organization there arise internal functional distinctions and internal stratification based upon them. Thus in the case of the Christian church, there developed the two orders: clergy and laity.

Religious Stratification
and Secular Stratification

What is the relation between the internal stratification of the religious organization and that of the general society? What is the relation between the clergy and the upper classes—the favored and the powerful—in society? Upon the answer to these questions depends the kind of relationship that develops between the church and society, the degree of conflict or accommodation involved, the degree of identification of the religious institution with the interests and stakes of various classes, the attitude of the church toward change and reform, etc.

The intricacy of the involvement of the church in society and of the internal stratification of the church with that of society may be seen in the Middle Ages. The society of that period evolved around two significant functions: the establishment and maintenance of order, and the provision of food and fibre. These two functions—ruling and fighting on the one hand, and agriculture on the other—gave rise to a stratification system which consisted of the nobility and gentry who ruled, fought, and supervised agricultural activity as lords of the manor, and the common people who worked in the fields and pursued the few skilled trades requisite to that society based upon meager technique. *Feudalism*—the relationships of reciprocal rights and duties which held together the upper classes—and *manorialism*—the super-

74

ordination-subordination relations between the gentle classes and the simple or peasant groups who were mostly serfs—evolved as the two main institutions of medieval society.

There was another institution in the society, the church. The church did not perform a function with respect to the environmental situation of the society; its basic task was neither ruling and fighting, nor raising crops. The church had come down from the earlier society, from the Roman Empire, and it performed a function based upon the religious purposes of the people, whom it had converted and taught. The clergy thus became an important class, performing what was generally considered the most important function. In this way there arose the three main classes of the early Middle Ages: the clergy, the nobility, and the common folk. With the rise of towns in the eleventh century a new function appeared—or, more accurately, an old function which had largely declined was revived. Commerce and the production of things for exchange developed, and with them cities and middle class groups. The new middle class found itself in conflict with the established order in its attempt to carve out a larger stake for itself in the medieval cities, in which it developed both commercial life and self-government.

In the medieval society, the church became the central and most influential institution. As a religious institution it was concerned with ultimate goals and values. Moreover, it still carried some of the prestige connected with antiquity, and before the thirteenth century churchmen were the only educated people. Consequently, the church had considerable moral and cultural ascendency, and religious values were central to the culture of European Christendom. The church had become an internally differentiated organization in which the clergy and the religious were the active core and the significant participants, and the lay people comprised the huge, passive periphery of "residual" and "second-class" members. *What was the relationship between the stratification of the society into aristocracy and simple folk, and the stratification of the church into clergy and laity?* There was in fact a good deal of "overlap" between the stratification systems of the church and the general society. The upper clergy (bishops, abbots, and other churchmen of influence) were largely drawn from the upper classes, as in fact was the membership of the monasteries, which were the most important religious groups at the time. It is true that the church did provide a very important avenue of social mobility to able young men from the lower classes, some of whom rose to great eminence in its ranks. But such upward mobility was always confined to small numbers. In Troeltsch's words, the upper clergy were "closely connected by ties of blood" to the nobility. Moreover, the church accumulated vast properties from gifts and bequests. Cathedrals, churches, and monasteries became deeply involved in the complex relationships of feudalism. As a consequence, the upper clergy and the upper classes of the feudal order were also tied together by ties of "mutual interests," to use another of Troeltsch's terms. The lower clergy were drawn from the lower classes, had inferior status, and often received quite meager rewards.

By the end of the eleventh century the new situation was already causing conflict in the cities. The new classes sought to improve their stake and

75

protested against existing conditions both in the towns and in the church. The church, involved in the feudal system, its upper clergy closely identified with the upper classes, "pressed heavily upon the lower classes and the inferior clergy" and consequently "there arose a vigorous opposition to the seignorial Church." [1] There thus arose a great social movement of the lower middle classes, comprised of people who hated a church "which treats the inferior clergy like serfs, which exploits the manorial rights through its tithes, which uses the wealth of the Church not for the poor, but for the Church itself, or for the feudal requirements of the higher clergy—a Church which in every respect is the opposite of the poverty of the apostles, and which, in contrast to the Early Church, excludes the congregation from every chance of cooperation." [2]

While there was developing in the towns an active opposition to the established order of things, there developed quite independently in the monasteries a protest against a general laxity in the church, and the breach and neglect of much ecclesiastical morality. This movement, which originated at the Benedictine monastery at Cluny, has been called the "cluniac reformation." It struck out against the marriage of priests, the selling of sacred things, and other abuses. In 1073, at a time when the agitation in the towns was developing into a great social movement, the reforming monk Hildebrand became pope, taking the name of Gregory VII. Thus the monastic reformation came together with the social movement in the towns.

The lower middle classes of the towns were reacting as deprived strata to the established order and as members of the laity to the condition of the church. They tended to see these as two aspects of the same situation, a situation which they interpreted to themselves in terms of their religious outlook and which they judged by religious and ethical standards. Pope Gregory instituted the so-called "Hildebrandine reform," and by his agitation stirred up the townspeople in its support. In the Lombard cities, for example, Troeltsch pointed out how "the laity arose in passionate struggles against the married clergy, with their simony, and in the infinite confusion which followed, when this order of clergy, banished by the Pope, was prevented from carrying out its functions, and when in every city bishops and priests were fighting against each other, and when there was often no one to conduct a service at all, this lay movement greatly increased." [3] The consequence was scepticism concerning the clergy and their functions, and a kind of anticlericalism which insisted upon the superiority of the layman.

Here we see religious and social issues merged, and religious and social interests united. What is the function of religion in this situation? On the one hand it sacralizes the privileged position of the established order and its leaders; on the other it provides the ideology and the leadership for protest. It provides the conceptualizations in terms of which the new classes can state and understand their protest, and the basis for justification of the protest in terms of religious values. Religion performs functions on both sides

[1] Ernst Troeltsch, *The Social Teachings of the Christian Churches*, Vol. I, trans. by Olive Wyon (New York: Macmillan, 1931), p. 349.
[2] *Loc. cit.*   [3] *Ibid.*, p. 350.

religion and conflict

of the conflict; its function in the situation is ambiguous. While religion provided the ideology which made it possible for new classes to develop and express their interests and their outlook, it also, by introducing sacred values into the issues, probably made the conflict more bitter.

There also evolved in this struggle a sectarian form of organization, as well as demands for reform of a marked sectarian character. To these sectarian aspects were added a religious doctrine which was heretical from a Christian point of view: the Gnostic-Manichaean, or Albigensian, heresy. This religious doctrine involved a radical dualism of spirit and matter and condemned the whole physical world as evil. Here we have an example of how social unrest and religious protest gave alien religious ideas a chance to become accepted in society. Once these ideas took hold among sections of the southern European population, they complicated the conflict tremendously. They took root in northern Italy and southern France, and had to be rooted out by fire and the sword. Pope Innocent III (1198–1216), a century after the events we have been considering, directed an armed crusade for twenty years to wipe out this heretical movement in Provence. Thus did religious ideas intensify conflicts whose origins lay in social and political differences in medieval society.

This eleventh century combination of social and religious conflict was a first rehearsal for the combination of religious and secular protest, the identification of religious ideologies and power drives, which later became so characteristic of the Reformation period. Said Troeltsch: "In this critical situation the excited laity was ripe to receive the inflammatory influence of an ancient sect, which was, it is true, in its dogma only semi-Christian, but which bore within its organization the sect-type of lay Christianity, and of criticism according to Scriptures and primitive Christian standards." [4] In fact, this early example of combined religious and social protest already evinced all the hallmarks of later religious revolt of the Reformation times.

> The effective elements of this movement were the free lay preaching, the criticism of the Church by the laity, the intimate fellowship of the scattered members, the practical example of poverty, indifference toward the State and the ruling classes, the rejection of the official Church and its priesthood, the refusal to swear in a court of law, or to have anything to do with the administration of justice, or with force, the abrogation of duties and tithes, the independent study of the Bible, and the habit of testing everything in Church life by the standards of the Primitive Church.[5]

We had seen earlier that the sect as a form of religious organization could arise as a response to anomie, providing both new values and a new sense of community to its participants. These elements are also visible in the case of the eleventh-century northern Italian cities. But this example also shows how the sect can be the expression of social as well as religious protest and opposition.

But as well as the "overlap" of religious and societal stratification—of religious and secular interests, which we have seen, and their ambiguous and confusing consequences—the inner stratification of the chruch and its rela-

4 *Loc. cit.*   5 *Ibid.*, p. 351.

tionship to the general society also had an opposite effect. Although the church was intricately intertwined with society, it was in some ways radically segregated from important aspects of the secular world. The rise of a professional clergy meant the evolution of a trained elite which would make the organizational interests and the separate welfare of the church its own most cherished concern. While it is true that the opposite tendency—the involvement of the upper clergy with the upper classes because of ties of blood and mutual interest—would often distract the clergy from this chief identification with the church, it is nevertheless true that on the whole this second tendency had great influence in European history.

In line with this second tendency came the development of the church into a clerical bureaucracy in which the laity were rendered peripheral and passive. Consistent with this organizational tendency was the doctrinal one which emphasized the other-worldly aspects of Christianity and saw little intrinsic value in the layman's this-worldly activities and goals. In ethics the church pursued a similar policy and held up to the laity what was in fact but a slightly modified form of the monastic ideal. The secular values of politics, commercial development, and economic affluence; learning for its own sake; the relationships of the sexes—these important human values might be exploited by the church for its own ecclesiastical ends, but they were never given full recognition in their own right. In all these realms of lay life, the lay classes of the medieval and early modern world asserted the autonomy of secular values against the recalcitrance, and often the open opposition, of churchmen. Consequently, from the fourteenth century on, the society of Europe (what had once been Christendom) seceded from the church and proclaimed the independence and autonomous worth of this-worldly values. An important contemporary Catholic theologian has said:

> During the middle ages the ecclesiastical institution included and formed human society; but from the beginning of the fourteenth century society began slowly to assert its independence. First to cut loose were rulers and their politics, then various activities of urban life and welfare, then thought and the sciences, then morality and spirituality itself, finally, and much more radically, the common consciousness of the people in their daily life of sorrows, joys, hope. . . . Now there was a kind of divorce between . . . a community of men who were hardly the faithful any longer and an institution of clerics whose problems, activities, interests, language were no longer those of the living human community.[6]

The relationship between religious and social stratification may be seen in America in a form somewhat different from that evident in Europe. The United States was settled by immigrants who came to this country over a long period of time. Those who came early by that very fact often got involved in important activities inherent in national development and became important groups with a considerable stake in the society. In this way Protestants of Anglo-Saxon stock tended to become the upper class groups and Protestantism tended to be the unofficially "established" religion of the

6 Yves M. J. Congar, O.P., *Lay People in the Church*, trans. by Donald Attwater (Westminster, Maryland: Newman Press, 1957), p. 41.

religion and conflict

American republic. Most of the immigrants who came after 1845 were not Protestants, but Catholics. As a consequence there has been a peculiar tendency toward the identification of religion with class position in America, an identification which only now, well into the second half of the twentieth century, is breaking down. Moreover, America is not the only area of the world where religious groups tend to coincide with ethnic groups and national communities. In the Middle East, where the Turks ruled minorities with the *millet* system which recognized a kind of political unity for religious communities, such groups tended to develop a general ethnic communal character.[7] And the end of British imperial rule in the Indian sub-continent saw the emergence, through much conflict and suffering, of India and Pakistan—two nations built upon religious identification. One example of the significance of this coincidence of religious and ethnic identities may be seen in America. Lipset and Bendix have pointed out how this complicates the study of certain important problems:

> In America the study of the relationship of social mobility to religious affiliation is complicated by the ethnic differences between Catholics and Protestants. Catholics comprise a much larger proportion of recent immigrants than do Protestants. Melville Dalton has suggested that foreign-born workers are less oriented toward occupational achievement than their native-born colleagues. Hence any examination of the differences in occupational achievement between American Catholics and Protestants should distinguish the effects of recent immigration from the impact of religious differences. Data collected by Samuel Stouffer indicate that occupational distribution of third-generation Catholics and Protestants differs from that of immigrants and the sons of immigrants, but that there is little or no difference between the occupational status achieved by third-generation Catholics and Protestants, except that more Protestants than Catholics are farmers.[8]

Religion can thus become intertwined with other elements in society in a complicated way. Religious ideas and religious values are in part influenced by the social groups among whom they originate; they express the needs, the thought-ways, the perspectives upon the world of such social strata. But once they become established as elements of the culture and are taught as the belief system of a religion, they have a formative influence upon the values and motivations of men. Thus religion is both affected by, and affects, social conditions. It can be either cause or effect.

This complicated interpenetration of religion and society has important implications for the study of religion. With the evolution of specifically religious organizations, religious bodies often become formal organizations and often develop bureaucratic structures. Such organizations have been fruitfully studied in terms of sociological theory developed in the field of formal organization. Strains, conflicts, and functional dilemmas common to other formal organizations are to be found in formal religious organizations as

---

[7] Werner J. Cahnman, "Religion and Nationality," in *Sociology and History*, Werner J. Cahnman and Alvin Boskoff (eds.) (New York: Free Press, 1964), pp. 271–279.

[8] Seymour Martin Lipset and Reinhard Bendix, *Social Mobility in Industrial Society* (Berkeley: University of California Press, 1959), pp 49–50.

well.[9] Since religious groups are often also ethnic groups, many important problems of relations between such groups and the general society and among such groups themselves may be studied effectively as problems of ethnic conflict, assimilation, and social mobility. A book such as Kenneth Underwood's *Protestant and Catholic* shows that a concrete study of the relations between and among religious groups in a community involves the examination of many elements to be found generally in intergroup relations and conflict, although in this case they are given their definite focus by the religious element.[10]

So far in this section we have seen the complex interrelation that may develop between religion and society, and also the ways in which religious organizations and religious interests may remain segregated from the general society and its activities and goals. We have seen that the function of religion may be highly ambiguous and that it may be involved on the two sides of important social conflicts. We have seen that religious ideas may aid new classes in defining their positions and aspirations, but that such religious definition may make conflict more extreme and lead it in a direction that makes compromise solution of problems impossible. Finally, the merger of the religious and secular elements is a fact from which we must take an important lesson: we must not take the obvious and manifest meaning of a religious conflict at its face value. Said Christopher Dawson, an eminent historian of Christianity: "Most of the great schisms and heresies in the history of the Christian Church have their roots in social and national antipathies, and if this had been clearly recognized by theologians the history of Christianity would have been a very different one." [11] The sociology of religion, as our analysis has shown, reveals this kind of significant latent level beneath the external appearances of diverse kinds of religious phenomena.

The Secularization of Culture

The ambiguities of the relation between religion and society, and the functions and dysfunctions of religion with respect both to society and to individuals, can be further examined by considering what is in fact the most outstanding social and cultural development of the last several centuries: *the secularization of culture*. In the course of this book so far we have noted several important things related to this process of secularization. We have seen that in primitive and traditional societies, religion is a pervasive matter, and that religious beliefs and rites play an important part in the activities of various kinds of groups, from the family to occupational groups. We have seen that in such societies, religion tends to provide the

---

[9] For example, most of the problems raised in two basic texts, Peter M. Blau and W. Richard Scott, *Formal Organizations* (San Francisco: Chandler Publishing Company, 1962) and Robert K. Merton, Ailsa P. Gray, Barbara Hockey and Hanan C. Selvin, *Reader in Bureaucracy* (Glencoe, Illinois: The Free Press, 1952), are found in religious organizations and especially in churches with hierarchical lines of authority.

[10] Kenneth Wilson Underwood, *Protestant and Catholic* (Boston: Beacon Press, 1957). See also John J. Kane, *Catholic-Protestant Conflicts in America* (Chicago: Regnery, 1955).

[11] Christopher Dawson, "Sociology as a Science," *Cross Currents* (Winter 1954), No. 2, 4:136.

religion and conflict

over-all point of view—the ideational system or complex of thought-ways—in whose context human experience in general is understood. In fact, for religious people in modern societies this is the case as well. We have also noted that specifically religious organizations evolve as part of the evolution of more urbanized societies with a greater degree of specialization in their activities. In our consideration of the development of theologies, we have pointed out how thought tends to go through a transformation from the mythic to the rational mode. Men come to be able to withhold emotional participation in their religious thinking and to develop systematic cognitive statements about their religious ideas. Furthermore, this rationalization of religious thought is part of a general process of the rationalization of thinking in general, which we noted developing in the ancient world. Finally, we saw that biblical religion introduced the conception of God as transcendent—as a "Thou" utterly above the world—and of the world as "desacralized," which is to say, no longer a sacred entity to be responded to with emotional involvement. Ancient Greek and Hebrew thinking tended to make the world an "it" to be manipulated both in thought and in action.

These considerations actually sum up significant aspects of the process of the secularization of culture. Secularization may be said to consist fundamentally of two related transformations in human thinking. There is first the *"desacralization"* of the attitude toward persons and things—the withdrawal of the kind of emotional involvement which is to be found in the religious response, in the response to the sacred. Secondly, there is the *rationalization of thought*—the withholding of emotional participation in thinking about the world. Rationalization implies both a cognitive attitude relatively free of emotion, and the use of logic rather than an emotional symbolism to organize thought. The secularization of culture, combining both desacralization and rationalization, means that a religious world-view is no longer the basic frame of reference for thought. Another view of the world as no longer sacred and composed of things to be manipulated comes into existence. This view more and more crowds the religious world-view into the sphere of "private" experience and becomes the mode of thought in the "public" sphere. Five kinds of human activity have been strategic in influencing the secularization of thought. Let us consider these briefly.

Work

The Bible begins its account of human history outside Eden with man sentenced to "till the ground" (Genesis 3:23) and to eat his bread by the sweat of his brow. (Genesis 3:19) Whatever their religious beliefs, their values, and their social structure, all men must meet the demands of their environment if their societies are to survive. "Evidently societies of men 'cannot live by bread alone.' But if 'every word that proceedeth out of the mouth of God' does not directly or indirectly promote the growth, the biological and economic prosperity of the society that sanctifies them, that society and its god with it will vanish ultimately." [12] Society's

[12] V. Gordon Childe, *What Happened in History* (New York: Penguin Books, 1946), p. 10.

growth and prosperity rest in the first place upon *work*—the application of intelligence and effort to satisfy human needs in meeting the demands of an environment. In relation to his environment, as Malinowski has said, primitive man "knows as well as you do that there are natural conditions and causes, and by his observations he knows also that he is able to control these natural forces by mental and physical effort." In these cases he resorts not to magic, "but to work, guided by knowledge and reason." [13] Primitive and archaic peoples develop empirical techniques of considerable technological sophistication. It is true that these often become traditionalized in a lore in which natural and supernatural elements, empirical techniques, and magical performance are intertwined in a complex body of tradition. Yet the practical demands involved in work could not but influence thinking in a realistic direction and thereby contribute to a diminution of the mythic and magical elements. This was true even in classical antiquity, when sophisticated thinking was separated by social cleavage from the world of work; the former the domain of leisured classes, the latter performed by people looked down upon as servile who in fact often were slaves. Greek medicine, Roman engineering and Roman agriculture, and the general state of military technology in antiquity suggest that even at that time "the separation of technics and science was [not] as complete as was sometimes supposed." [14] And when technical experience affects science, it enters into the general thinking of a culture and affects its world view.

In Europe in the Middle Ages many practical technical innovations, from the stirrup, the horse collar, and the heavy plow to windmills and techniques of mining, were invented or else borrowed from other societies. Moreover, in that period the thinking of educated men and the practical activities of men at work were never "totally divorced," and as time went on "their association became more intimate." [15] As a consequence of a continual advance in technology, "as early as 1300, Western Christendom was using many techniques either unknown or undeveloped in the Roman Empire. By the year 1500 the most advanced countries of the West were in most aspects of technics distinctly superior to any earlier society." [16] In modern times Western man has developed a great technological revolution in production and communication, which has radically altered his relationship to his environment and brought his control over natural forces to hitherto undreamed-of heights.

The consequence of man's successful achievement in the sphere of work is a society in which things are more plentiful, events more predictable, and natural forces more under human control. In other words, technological development in the sphere of work has reduced the impact upon human experience of the three elements which we earlier saw as closely related to the functions of religion—contingency, powerlessness, and scarcity. The need for

<hr />

[13] Bronislaw Malinowski, *Magic, Science and Religion* (Garden City, N.Y.: Doubleday Anchor Books, 1954), p. 28. See Chapter One above, p. 8.
[14] A. C. Crombie, *Medieval and Early Modern Science*, Vol. I (Cambridge, Mass.: Harvard University Press, 1959), p. 175.
[15] *Loc. cit.*   [16] *Ibid.*, pp. 188–189.

religion and conflict

the related functions of religion was thereby reduced. This remains substantially the case despite the new dangers deriving from nuclear weapons in a world lacking adequate social controls. Moreover, men learned through this successful betterment of their control over their environment to achieve security through active manipulation of natural elements and forces, rather than finding it in a religious relationship. They learned to turn mysteries into problems; to substitute an "I-It" attitude for an "I-Thou" attitude.

War

Men have faced not only difficult and recalcitrant natural environments, but hostile and threatening human ones as well. War has played an important role in human history as both a means of defense and a method of aggrandizement. In war, as in work, men learned to apply themselves practically, and to achieve mastery over their environment. Of course, in war, as in work, they supplemented empirical technique with magical incantation. Reality submitted all their efforts to the pragmatic test. War very often provided that stark, this-worldly necessity which is the mother of invention, and out of necessity often came further means to control the environment, means that were later applied to the sphere of work. Military engineering was the first engineering specialty; military mass-production the first form of mass-production. War was indeed for a long time "the chief propagator of the machine." [17]

Exchange

A third sphere of human activity that has been of great importance to the rationalization of thought is that of *economic activity*. In traditional societies, the allocation of goods is largely governed by the non-economic relations of men—their status in kinship groups or other non-utilitarian forms of human organization. Closely related to the specialization of function which is characteristic of the change from traditional to modern societies is the development of exchange. This exchange tends over time to become increasingly separated from traditional social status. A *market* develops in which men exchange goods, frankly seeking recognized advantage, and subject only to established rules of honesty and procedure. *Contract* replaces *status* as the basis for distribution. The development of a market—of contractual relationships governing exchange—enhanced the development of rational calculation and long-term rational action. Said Max Weber, 'One of the most important aspects of the process of 'rationalization' of action is the substitution for the unthinking acceptance of ancient custom, of deliberate adaptation to situations in terms of self-interest." [18]

The development of commerce and the rise of middle classes during the Middle Ages were part of this process. In Italy, during the twelfth and thirteenth centuries, Italian business firms opened branches in France, the

[17] Lewis Mumford, *Technics and Civilization* (New York and Burlingame: Harcourt, Brace and World, 1963), p. 86.
[18] Max Weber, *The Theory of Social and Economic Organization*, trans. by A. M. Henderson and Talcott Parsons, Talcott Parsons (ed.) (New York: Oxford University Press, 1947), p. 123.

religion and conflict

Netherlands, England, and the Middle East. In this great expansion of trade, the "making of a decent living, which remained the chief purpose of men engaged in local commerce even in Italy, was replaced by the calculating pursuit of profit with a view to reinvestment and accumulation of wealth." [19] Personal management in these large firms was replaced by methods of administration and exchange—correspondence and letters of credit, for example —which comprised the fundamental techniques of merchant capitalism. Market relationships based upon money rather than status marked a considerable desacralization of traditional human relationships. Rationalized and expanded commerce represented a breaking down of provincial ways of thought. The pursuit of economic gain by methods involving rational calculation and action meant a great advance in human mastery over environmental conditions Thus early capitalism contributed to the process of secularization.

Government

A fourth sphere of human activity in which a diminution of the sacred and a rationalization of thought and action took place is that of *government and law*. With the growth of larger political units like the empires of antiquity or the dynastic states of the Middle Ages and early modern times, or in the context of the universal church with its problems of government and administration, legal and administrative activitie had to become more coordinated and hence more rational. Codified law itself the beginning of rational consistency in handling important human problems, developed early in Babylon, Greece, Rome, and elsewhere. Yet ir the ancient empires of the East, bureaucratic administration did not change men's outlook sufficiently to alter seriously the traditional view of the world Despite a rationality of procedure, the world-views of such cultures remained largely mythic in character. In Rome, however, law of a rational characte reached a high development.[20]

This law was revived in the Middle Ages and became the model fo adjudication and administration, and indeed the basis for much of medieva thinking about human relations and human society. It had tremendou formative influence upon the law of Europe, the canon law of the church and even on law in England, where however it failed to oust the commor law from its central position. In medieval Europe, the Roman law "wa crudely taken and then painfully learned, till in the end, vitally and broadl mastered, it became even a means and mode of medieval thinking." [21] I early modern times, the Roman law provided monarchs and popes a mode for government and administration, as well as for adjudication. Roman law revived in the context of practical governmental problems of both civil an church governments, represents a genuine rationalization of thought. I "established in the Western mind the ideal that an authority should be a once lawful, and law-enforcing, and should in itself exhibit a rationally ad

[19] Wallace K. Ferguson, *The Renaissance* (New York: Henry Holt, 1951), p. 46.
[20] H. O. Taylor, *The Mediaeval Mind*, 4th ed. (Cambridge, Mass.: Harvard University Press, 1959), p. 261. [21] *Ibid.*, p. 260.

84

religion and conflict

usted system of organization." [22] Moreover, in providing norms derived from reason and experience, it gave thinking about government and human relations a decidedly this-worldly direction. While law remained sacred in some sense, it was in the diminished sense of the sacredness which Weber attributes to the charisma of office. Actually, rational law and administration contributed significantly to the secularization of thought and action.

Learning and Science

A fifth sphere in which developing secularization proceeds is to be seen in the context of intellectual life—the realm of learning and science. Men are not merely practical in their thinking; they also desire answers to questions posed by their curiosity, and by the problem of ultimate meaning. Interpretations of man, cosmogonies, and explanations of human destiny are to be found in all cultures. In Chapter Three we saw how these tend to become increasingly rationalized. This transformation, while probably inherent in the development of thought itself, tends to be supported and facilitated by general social and cultural conditions. In theology, the emergence of a class of professional clergy was seen to be one important precondition of rationalization. Science and philosophy began in the Greek cities of Ionia, where trade, with its depersonalization of exchange, and urban life, with its replacement of village parochialism with a more varied environment, had taken place. It was an environment where men could think about themselves and their world in a more rational manner.

In ancient Babylonia, Assyria, and Egypt, and in ancient India and China as well, a large-scale and effective technology had developed. It remained true, however, that this practical accomplishment "was unaccompanied by any conception of scientific explanation." Babylonian cuneiform texts, for example, present accurate methods of predicting the movements of the stars, but offer no natural explanation for such phenomena. A. C. Crombie, a distinguished historian of science, has said: "The texts in which they set out to 'explain' the world, as distinct from predicting its happenings, contain myths in which the visible order of things is attributed to a legal system obeyed by arbitrary choice by a society of gods personifying natural forces." [23]

In Greece, however, men really invented scientific thought. From this Hellenic beginning came both philosophy and science. Philosophy became the realm of rational thinking concerning the meaning of life and experience and contributed much to rationalization and the desacralization of thought. Science made similar contributions and in recent times became the means of achieving tremendous mastery over natural forces, a fact of fundamental significance for the development of secularization. It was the French philosopher, René Descartes (1596–1650), who proclaimed that science would make man "the master and possessor of nature." In advancing men in this direction, science has also contributed to a change in human thinking. The

[22] Alfred North Whitehead, Science and the Modern World (New York: The Macmillan Company; Cambridge University Press, 1948), p. 15.
[23] Crombie, op. cit., pp. 4–5.

world is desacralized; it is an "It" to be controlled for human purposes. Modern man has developed what might be called "the problem-solving mentality," the derivative of the process of secularization.

Werner Sombart, in his study of the quintessence of capitalism, saw on the one hand the capitalist spirit, compounded of greed for gold, desire for adventure, and love of exploration, and on the other the bourgeois spirit, made up of rational calculation and economy. The secularization of culture in the five spheres we have discussed obviously helped to bring about many of these component attitudinal elements. They found their expression in grand dimensions in the development of empire, the expansion of commerce, and the discovery and exploration of new continents and oceans in the early modern period.

In Chapter Three we have already examined the process of secularization as it took place within religion itself. We noted how the Judeo-Christian conception of God as transcendent desacralized the world; how it prepared the attitude necessary to approach the world as an empirical "It" rather than a sacred "Thou." The conception in the same tradition which sees God as rational as well as personal implied the scrutability of nature and its knowability by man, made in God's image. The trust in reason upon which modern scientific development rested was an "unconscious derivative from medieval theology." [24] The evolution of an idea of the world no longer sacred, and one understandable by human reason, means the emergence of a world where *mysteries are replaced by problems.* It is the development of a secularized understanding of man and his situation. Along with it developed a middle class confidence in human effort deriving from success, and among some strata an exuberant enthusiasm for what is new.

Religion and Secularization:
Ambiguity and Conflict

The secularization of culture involved both a diminution of the sacred and an increase in rationality in the thinking of men. It was both a metamorphosis of thought and a transformation of society for it involved changes in both the modes of thinking and the basic activities of men, and consequently in the social structure of society. Urban societies devoted to this-worldly activities developed as the structural base for changes in the forms and modes of thinking. The evolution of an urban society, built first on commerce and later on industry, was fundamentally an anti-traditionalist development. The emergence of a secular culture was basically an anti-religious or at least "counter-religious" development. Yet both these statements require considerable qualification. City life often tended to become traditionalized again; religion often aided secularization and adopted aspects of its point of view. Indeed, as we have already seen not all religions opposed all aspects of secularization. Most of the world religions have undergone some degree of rationalization and have thus contributed to secularization. Biblical religion which desacralized the world was

[24] Whitehead, *op. cit.*, p. 14.

religion and conflict

an important factor in the secularization of Western thought. It is therefore impossible to generalize very far on the relations between religion and secularization in the abstract. What is necessary is to examine particular religions and their reactions to particular aspects of the secularization process. The Christian church, as we have already seen, made a partial acceptance of Greek rationality. Moreover, its conviction of the reality of human history and the seriousness of life in this world, as contained and implied in the Bible, tended to support this-worldly action over the long run, despite the always predominant other-worldly emphasis of Christian values. In compromising with the world and accepting culture, the church accepted and indeed often advanced aspects of secularization. Out of the Church had come the medieval universities, and in the universities there developed creative and controversial thinking and a continual reappropriation of antique culture, both important elements in advancing secularization. Yet the conflict between faith and reason was as characteristic of intellectual life in the Middle Ages as it has been in modern times. Moreover, the clergy possessed a monopoly of intellectual matters in the Middle Ages, and the church attempted to restrain thinking to keep it within the bounds of orthodoxy by control of university curricula and later through the institution of inquisitions. Yet the universities became the scene of vigorous dialogue and debate on the most fundamental issues in philosophy and theology. In the thoroughly religious medieval city, there was a great increase in anti-clericalism and in what historians have called the "lay spirit," a sentiment affirming the worth of the layman and the value of his this-worldly activity and interests. Yet as the great Belgian historian of the Middle Ages, Henri Pirenne, has pointed out, this lay spirit "was allied with the most intense religious fervor." [25] The result was innovation and heresy, and conflict with ecclesiastical authority, which at times was defending the orthodoxy of faith, at times the vested interests of office holders. Both novelty and conflict contributed to advancing secularization. Pirenne concludes his study with these words:

> Both lay and mystic at the same time, the burghers of the Middle Ages were thus singularly well prepared for the role which they were to play in the two great future movements of ideas: the Renaissance, the child of the lay mind, and the Reformation, toward which religious mysticism was leading.[26]

In the more developed and affluent cities of the Italian Renaissance a secular spirit grew markedly among the upper classes. These classes were "consciously and rationally preoccupied with the pursuit of this world's goods." Their wealth "enabled them to enjoy the pleasures of this world" and they drifted away "from the ascetic otherworldliness which monastic ideology had made so strong an element in medieval religion." They no longer experienced the world as "a vale of tears" and they became "less willing to allow the clergy to do their thinking for them, or to permit the church to control economic and social activities that they felt could be handled more

[25] Henri Pirenne, *Medieval Cities* (Garden City, N.Y.: Doubleday Inc., 1956), pp. 166–67.
[26] *Ibid.*, p. 167.

religion and conflict

satisfactorily by their own state governments."[27] Although religious belief remained strong, the Renaissance saw a great increase in the secularization of life and thought. What began in Italy spread to the northern countries.

What was the role of the church with respect to this complex secularization process? It was, as we have seen, a varied one, a many-sided one, a contradictory one. The church was both sponsor and opponent. The highly religious life of the medieval university and the medieval city, so much a product of the ideas of Christianity, was the locus of considerable secularization and prepared for the more marked secularization of the Renaissance. The church sponsored activities in intellectual life, in art, in political life, and even in business, which hastened and contributed to this process. But the church also stood in opposition. Sometimes the church and churchmen opposed aspects of the secularization process because they genuinely threatened the Christian religion or represented action the church deemed unethical; sometimes because they infringed upon quite secular interests of churchmen or the ecclesiastical institution.

Medieval intellectual life is replete with incidents of conflict between those who pursued knowledge and those in authority who would restrain such activity, from St. Bernard's thunderings against Abelard to the condemnation of the ideas of St. Thomas Aquinas by ecclesiastical synods in France and England. In economic life in both the Middle Ages and early modern times, the church—and after the Reformation both its Catholic and Protestant branches—opposed economic activity in pursuit of gain outside the context of ethical reciprocities of a more or less traditional kind. R. H. Tawney, in his famous work, *Religion and the Rise of Capitalism*, summarizes the Christian view in this way:

> Labor—the common lot of mankind—is necessary and honorable; trade is necessary, but perilous to the soul; finance, if not immoral, is at best sordid and at worst disreputable. . . . The suspicion of economic motives had been one of the earliest elements in the social teaching of the Church, and was to survive till Calvinism endowed the life of economic enterprise with a new sanctification.[28]

This point of view was not limited to the pre-Reformation church or to post-Reformation Catholicism. The manifest teachings of Protestantism as well as Catholicism were opposed to the early development of a capitalism freed of social and ethical restraints on economic self-interest. In Europe, "the spirit of capitalism is foreign to every kind of religion."[29] Said the continental reformer Bucer, in his *De Regno Christi:* "Neither the Church of Christ, nor a Christian Commonwealth, ought to tolerate such as prefer private gain to the public weal, or seek it to the hurt of their neighbor."

[27] Ferguson, *op. cit.*, pp. 67–70. For an interesting analysis of changes in the culture and social structure of Europe at this time, see Alfred von Martin, *Sociology of the Renaissance* (New York: Oxford University Press, 1944).

[28] R. H. Tawney, *Religion and the Rise of Capitalism* (New York: Harcourt, Brace & World, 1947), pp. 36–37.

[29] Kurt Samuelsson, *Religion and Economic Action*, trans. by E. Geoffrey French (New York and Evanston: Harper Torchbooks, 1964), p. 19.

88

religion and conflict

In the political sphere, the church contributed to the advance of rationalization by its acceptance of the Roman law and by its rationalization of procedures in its own internal administration. Yet in this realm of life, both in the Middle Ages and modern times, the struggle of the church with the secular state was an important cause of conflict. The church fought civil governments both to defend its own independence and to protect its own secular interests. At times the church threatened the autonomy of secular governments themselves. Political thought and legal philosophy reflected this conflict of points of view and interest and transmitted it to future generations to re-enact it once more in their own time.

In all these areas of human action the relation of Christianity and of the Christian church to the secularization of culture was an intricate and ambiguous one. Nowhere is the complexity, ambiguity, and dysfunctionality of the church's relation to secularization to be seen so clearly as in the development of science. The church's early acceptance of rationality, its role in the preservation and rediscovery of ancient culture, its patronage of learning—all these contributed to the formation of the preconditions for the rise of modern science in a most significant way. Moreover, churchmen and devout laymen played a crucial role in the early history of science. But science—first astronomy, then physics, and much later biology—tended to undermine and throw into disarray the highly explicit and semi-mythical ideas which informed the church's doctrines concerning the origin and pre-history of the earth. Consequently, the church found itself fighting against science. In the words of the Frenchman Lecomte du Noüy, a Christian who was also a scientist:

> The Church progressively became a vast administrative machine, jealous of its prerogatives and its authority, convinced of its infallibility even in questions unrelated to dogma. When it encountered individuals who dared to think independently in certain fields, it often looked on them with a suspicious eye. . . . The clergy should have understood that all attacks on freedom of thought, when neither morals nor dogma were concerned, made enemies of the very people it most needed. The Church became frightened; it doubted.[30]

Although the significance of the case of Galileo has undoubtedly been granted exaggerated importance by later commentators, it nevertheless remains the great symbol of religious opposition to the advance of science. The Congregation of the Index, a department of the Roman Curia, the administrative organ of the Pope as supreme ruler of the Roman Catholic Church, in 1616 prepared and promulgated a decree declaring the heliocentric thesis in astronomy to be formally heretical in the eyes of the church, and ordered Galileo not to maintain it or treat it in any way. In 1633, the Congregation of the Inquisition or the Holy Office, the Congregation of the Curia charged with maintaining orthodoxy and protecting religious belief, sentenced Galileo as "vehemently suspected of heresy for having held and believed the doctrine,

---

[30] Lecomte du Noüy, *The Road to Reason*, trans. and ed. by Mary Lecomte du Noüy (New York: Longmans, 1948), pp. 207–208.

which is false and contrary to Holy Scripture, that the sun is the center of the world."[31] While he was not subjected to physical torture or abuse, as has sometimes been asserted in the myth that grew up around this archetypal case, and although the Inquisition did not speak for the highest teaching authority of the church, the fact remains that Galileo was condemned as a scientist pursuing science. Thus crystallized the lines of conflict between science and religion which were to mark off the battleground for three centuries to come.

Later in the seventeenth century, both science and the secularization of thought took on great dimensions. Even at the beginning of that century it has been estimated that in Paris—a city of some 300,000 people—there were about 50,000 atheists.[32] In the eighteenth century, the upper classes of western Europe become largely secularized. The combination of social mobility of lower middle class groups, who had remained religious, and movements within Christianity (such as Wesleyanism, which proselytized among the working classes, whom industrialization was uprooting from the older rural cultural settings) brought about a betterment of the position of religion in the nineteenth century. "But today, when modern education has infiltrated the ideas of modern science and of new practicality into the minds of common men, and when for the first time in history even powerful states have taken up an open fight against religion—today religion is in critical danger."[33] Since World War II, in both America and Europe, there has been a degree of religious revival, on both the popular and intellectual levels. There also has been a recognition among religious leaders that religion is in danger of being judged irrelevant by men in today's dynamic society, which is based upon technological revolution in production and communication. Pope John XXIII, in calling the Second Vatican Council and initiating the program to update the Catholic church, has offered the most dramatic example of this recognition. The threat of secularization, however, is still seen by most religious leaders in the West as a grave danger, and the tension between religion and secularization remains one of the significant sources of conflict in the western world today.

Five Dilemmas
in the Institutionalization of Religion

The dysfunctions of religion, the ambiguities of the relationship between religion and society, and the contribution of religion to the creation and exacerbation of social conflict are all complicated by the fact that the institutionalization of religion is itself the working out of a set of structurally inherent dilemmas. Five such dilemmas may be distinguished as characteristic of the development of specifically religious organizations, and from these derive many of the internal strains and functional problems

[31] Charles Journet, *The Church of the Word Incarnate*, Vol. I (New York: Sheed and Ward, 1955), p. 355.
[32] Erich Frank, *Philosophical Understanding and Religious Truth* (New York: Oxford University Press, 1952), p. 5.
[33] *Ibid.*, p. 260.

religion and conflict

of such religious bodies. These five paradoxes of institutionalization are discussed below. [34]

The Dilemma of Mixed Motivation

In the first or charismatic period in the development of founded religions, usually to be seen in the relationship between a charismatic leader and his disciples, the motivation of the active participants tends to be characterized by considerable single-mindedness. The religious movement does satisfy complex needs for its adherents, but such needs are focused upon religious values as these are proclaimed and embodied by the charismatic leader. With institutionalization, however, an important innovation is introduced.

Institutionalization involves a stable set of statuses and roles, defined in terms of functions, upon which are encumbent rights and obligations. There arises a structure of offices which involves a stratified set of rewards in terms of prestige, life opportunities, and material compensations.

This process is clearly to be observed in the emergence of specifically religious organizations. The stable structure which thus develops becomes capable of eliciting a wide range of individual motives and of focusing diverse motivations behind the goals of the organization as specified in prescribed role behavior. This process has the strategic functional significance of providing stability, since the organization no longer has to depend upon disinterested motivation. Institutionalization mobilizes behind institutionalized expectations what Parsons has called both disinterested and interested motivation. However, this mobilization of a variety of motives in support of the goals and values of the organization can, and often does, result in the subtle transformation of the goals and values themselves. When a professional clergy emerges in the church, there comes into existence a body of men for whom the clerical life offers not simply the "religious" satisfactions of the earlier charismatic period, but also prestige and respectability, power and influence, in both church and society, and satisfactions derived from the use of personal talents in teaching, leadership, etc. Moreover, the *maintenance* of the situation in which these rewards are forthcoming tends to become an element in the motivation of the group.

We have already seen numerous examples of the kinds of changes which such developments introduce into the church and the way that they affect the relationship of the church and society. The higher clergy in Christian history became important functionaries and dignitaries in society, with all the rewards and benefits accruing to people in such positions. The higher clergy, in terms of both church office and of non-ecclesiastical governmental functions, became part of the ruling and dominant classes in society, and their interests fused with those of such classes. These new interests of the

[34] These five dilemmas are treated at somewhat greater length in two articles, "Five Dilemmas in the Institutionalization of Religion," *Journal for the Scientific Study of Religion* (October 1961), No. 1, I:30–39; and "Sociological Dilemmas: Five Paradoxes of Institutionalization," in *Sociological Theory, Values and Sociocultural Change*, Edward A. Tiryakian (ed.) (New York: Free Press of Glencoe, 1963), pp. 71–89.

91

clergy often deviated from the goals and values of the church. The church was transformed in a subtle way. It became secularized; the clergy became "worldly." Since it is the clergy who interpret the church's teachings, these come to be understood and applied in ways which tend to express and maintain the interests of the clerical stratum itself. Thus while mixed motivation, introduced by institutionalization, enhances stability and contributes to the survival of the organization, it also represents a source of serious transformation in the goals and values of the church.

This development of mixed motivation is most significant with respect to leadership roles, but it is to be seen in the rank and file as well. As "born members" replaced people who had been converted, a different kind of motivation and identification came to prevail in the church. As the laity became a more passive element in the church, lay people tended to develop a different kind of identification, and their motives for participation changed as well. Already in the second century there appears a prophetic literature denouncing the resulting lukewarmness of many in the church.

The Symbolic Dilemma: Objectification versus Alienation

We have seen that the cultic re-presentation of the religious experience is central to the life of the religious group, and that it is a symbolic performance. As an embodiment of religious meanings and as the means of acting out religious attitudes, the symbol becomes subject to the strains and dilemmas embodied in religion itself. To retain the original experience, with its supraempirical relation to the ultimate and the sacred, it must be given expression in symbolic forms which are themselves empirical and profane, and which with repetition become prosaic and everyday in character. Hence the use of symbols in order to make possible "a prolongation of hierophanies," [35] or apprehensions of the sacred, can be a first step in routinization.

Susanne Langer has pointed out that ritual is expressive in a logical rather than in a psychological sense.[36] Ritual represents an objectified order of symbols which elicits and articulates attitudes and feelings, molding the personal dispositions of the worshipers after its own model. This objectification is a requisite for continuity, and for sharing within the religious group. Without such objectification and sharing, collective worship would be impossible. Yet a continued use of the same symbolic vehicles has the effect of making them usual and expected—that is, of routinizing them. The necessary objectification tends to remove the symbols from meaningful contact with subjective attitudes. Thus there develops a loss of resonance between the symbol and the attitudes and feelings from which it originally derived. The symbol consequently loses its power to elicit and affect attitudes and emotions. Objectification, necessary for continuity, leads finally to alienation.

The history of religion offers many examples of this process of the

---

[35] Mircea Eliade, *Patterns in Comparative Religion*, trans. by Rosemary Sheed (New York: Sheed and Ward, 1958), p. 448.
[36] See Chapter Three above, pp. 39ff.

religion and conflict

alienation of symbols. In the Middle Ages, people lost the sense of the original meaning of much of the symbolism involved in the Mass. It then became necessary for churchmen to invent an elaborate secondary allegorization, attributing novel and often extrinsic meanings to the alienated symbols. A kind of charisma of the obscure may be maintained by the development of archaism, as in the use of a little-understood dead language, special apparel, and a stylization of performance. But such secondary reactions to alienation do not change the basic situation. The embodiment of the sacred in the profane vehicle causes a loss of sacredness. The embodiment of the ultimate in empirical symbols causes a diminution of the sense of ultimacy itself. Repetition robs ritual of its unusual character, so significant for charisma, and routinizes it. The loss of resonance means the loss of the original emotional meaning. The symbolic order thus becomes alienated. Cult, dependent upon symbolism, then is reduced to a routine performance of established formalities, and no longer serves its original purpose.

This alienation of symbolism and the evolution of a charisma of the obscure gives rise to protest. The importance of both to the anti-symbolic reactions of the left-wing of the Reformation can hardly be overestimated. The more extreme Protestant groups attacked the Mass with great bitterness, broke stained-glass windows, removed altars and statues from churches, and violently desecrated the sacrament. Such symbolic expressions of the older church were seen as idols and as barriers in the way of the religious experience, rather than as elements promoting and eliciting it. Thus was religious solidarity weakened and violent protest evoked.

The Dilemma of Administrative Order: Elaboration and Alienation

The routinization of charisma often gives rise to formal organization with bureaucratic structure. New offices tend to develop as new functions arise. Moreover, precedents established in action lead to a transformation of existing offices. The general contours of the administrative structure tend to reflect the problems and functions in response to which the structure developed. There are several factors which tend to render such bureaucratic structures dysfunctional. Structures which emerge in one set of conditions and in response to one set of problems may turn out later to be unwieldly instruments for handling new problems under new conditions. Functional precedents established in handling earlier problems can become dysfunctional in later situations, and can even become formidable obstacles blocking any forthright action.

Since it is this structure of offices which becomes the mechanism for eliciting the mixed motivation we have discussed above, and mobilizing it behind organizational goals, the individuals involved come to have a vested interest in the structure as it is, and to resist change and reform, which they tend to see as threatening to themselves. Thus not only can the structure become overelaborated and alienated from contemporary problems, but it can contribute to the alienation of office holders from the rank-and-file members of the group. Such developments are clearly visible in the history of the

93

church. They were intensified by the rediscovery and appropriation of Roman law, which provided the church with a rational-legal bureaucratic model. The frustration of efforts to reform the church in the two centuries before Luther; the rise of clericalism; the conflict between bishops and bureaucrats of the Roman Curia—all are examples of the effects of this dilemma, as it is complicated by the development of mixed motivation.

The Dilemma of Delimitation: Concrete Definition versus Substitution of the Letter for the Spirit

To affect the lives of men, the original religious message must be stated in terms that have relevance to the everyday activities and concerns of people. Moreover, to preserve the import of the message, it must be protected against interpretations which would transform it in ways conflicting with its inner ethos. These needs are characteristic of both the religious message and the ethic implied in it. Both of these needs constitute a strong pressure for definition. Thus in the history of the Christian church we see a continual process in which doctrine is defined in response to interpretations felt to be heretical. Moreover, with respect to the Christian ethic, it was soon found that its implications had to be spelled out in some detail for the new converts made among the gentiles. This involved both the utilization of elements of Hebraic law—the Ten Commandments, especially, which Paul had considered as superseded—and the natural law of Greek philosophy, especially as formulated by the Stoics. Such definition was also a process of concretization, and it was a functional necessity without which the church could hardly have maintained its religious insights and its organizational integrity.

This process of definition and concretization is at the same time a relativization of the religious and ethical message—a rendering of it relevant to the new circumstances of life of the religious group—and therefore involves the risk of making everyday and prosaic what was originally a call to the extraordinary. Moreover, implications drawn in concrete form under particular circumstances may come to be accepted in a literalist manner, in which the original scope of the implications of the religious message may be lost. The problem may be seen quite clearly in the sphere of the religious ethic. The original ethical insight is translated into a set of rules to bring it within the grasp of new converts. These rules give the original ethical insight a kind of "operational definition" comprehensible to the average man. Yet rules, however elaborate they may become, cannot make explicit all that was implied in the original insight itself, and run the risk of losing its spirit. Rules specify, and thereby substitute for the original insight specific items of prescribed or proscribed behavior. Thus there can develop a complicated set of legalistic formulations. In Hinduism this process may be seen in the evolution of elaborate proscriptions to preserve ritual purity. It may also be seen in the Pharisaic rituals in Judaism of the classical period. Both Catholicism and Protestantism show signs of this rigorism in their histories. Here, indeed, as St. Paul put it, "the letter killeth, but the spirit giveth life."

94

The problem is not, however, limited to the sphere of ethics. The threat and challenge of heresy led to a continual definition of dogma as the required canon of faith in the Roman Catholic Church. This gave rise to a complicated, difficult, and subtle statement of doctrines beyond the competence of those not trained in the theological tradition. Such definitions bear the marks of the conflicts out of which they have arisen and the cultural meanings current at the time. In the Catholic church, once such definitions are made, they are unalterable, and such areas are closed to new thought and definition. This fact has been and will continue to be a serious source of conflict within the church and between the church and other groups in society. Even when the defined precedents may not be of the highest dogmatic status, the importance of definition can cause serious difficulty. This may be seen in the conflict within the church concerning birth control in the light of the church's moral teachings.

While the dangers of distortion of the faith of the church require these definitions of dogma and morals, once established, the definitions themselves pose the possibility of another kind of distortion. They become a vast intellectual structure which serves not to guide the faith of untrained specialists but rather to burden it. Moreover, since such a technically spelled-out content of faith requires the interpretation of specialists, the gulf between clergy and laity is thereby maintained. There is danger that an intellectual assent to authority is substituted for the more holistic act of faith.

Closely related to both this dilemma of delimitation and to the dilemma of the objectification and alienation of symbols is that form of the degeneration of symbols which the great student of religion, Mircea Eliade, calls "a process of infantilization." [37] In this infantilization, the symbol becomes "mechanistic and crude." It is often "taken in a childish way, overconcretely, and apart from the system it belongs to." Eliade points out that this can develop in the "descent" of the symbol "from a scholarly to a popular level." It can also come about by the symbol becoming "a substitute for the sacred object" or "a means of establishing a relationship with it." The symbols, when they are thus converted into means, become magical or quasi-magical in character. Eliade comments that this phenomenon of the infantilization of symbolism is to be found "not only among 'primitives,' but even in the most developed societies." The philosopher, Karl Jaspers, also speaks of magic of this kind as the ever-present perversion in which "the reality of the symbol becomes a purposive and instrumental technique." [38] An example of this infantilism of discursive symbolism may be seen in biblical fundamentalism in which an over-concrete and extremely literal understanding of biblical texts, outside the context of any historical, theological, or linguistic frame of reference, becomes the rule of religious faith. It is a development that became of considerable importance in American Protestantism. The use of sacred objects as charms, and of prayers as magical rituals, offer other examples of infantilization with presentational as well as verbal symbols.

---

[37] Eliade, *op. cit.*, pp. 444 and 456.
[38] Karl Jaspers, "Freedom and Authority," *Diogenes* (Winter 1953), 1:33.

The Dilemma of Power:
Conversion versus Coercion

The religious experience exercises a call, and thereby mobilizes the inner dispositions of the person called to a voluntary adherence to religious leaders, beliefs, and movements. It involves that commitment of the individual which may be called the "act of faith." But faith as a commitment to the supraempirical involves the possibility of doubt. When the religious organization becomes institutionalized and accommodates itself to the society and its values, faith is supplemented by public opinion and current ideas of respectability. More precisely, faith is supplemented by consensual validation and by the approval and support of accepted authority. The result is that a specious obviousness tends to develop and render the content of faith commonplace. The content of faith tends to be accepted without examination, but is therefore vulnerable to questions when they do arise. Moreover, the compromise of religion with culture—with the "world" in Troeltsch's sense—tends to make religion the repository of the basic values of the society. Thus not only are religious beliefs made more vulnerable to questioning, but they are also functionally more significant to secular society. Faith and doubt remain closely related, and beneath the institutionalized "self-evidentness," the basic structure of religion and of society's legitimation remains vulnerable to questioning—questioning which dispels the consensually derived but only apparent obviousness of beliefs.

The ever present vulnerability of faith to doubt makes religious leaders tend to rely upon social consensus and even on legal authority to buttress and supplement voluntary adherence. Society's leaders, needing religion to sanctify society's values and support social control, tend to protect religion and religious institutions from threat. Thus there arises the possibility of an alignment of religious and secular authorities. This situation, as may be seen in the history of Christianity, draws religious and secular power together to enforce religious conformity. The heretic and the unbeliever weaken consensus and pose a social threat. Those weak in faith tend to project their own potential and half-conscious doubts onto the unbeliever, and then persecute him. Such "ritualistic" purgings of self have taken place both legally—that is, within the orderly and often careful procedures of courts of inquisition—and illegally, by mob action and other violent forms of attack. Thus intolerance and persecution come to perform two functions. For the society, they reinforce and protect a religion, and through the religion the society and its values, from the undermining of doubt. For individuals, they offer a way of externalizing their own doubts and striking at them in the persons of others. Yet it may be questioned whether indeed these functions are performed without quite negative unintended consequences. The consensus that is built upon or supported by threats of force is one to which genuine adherence is gradually weakened. The reliance upon power to supplement faith violates an important element of the religious experience upon which religious institutions ultimately rest: its spontaneous and voluntary character.

A genuine dilemma is involved. Religion cannot but relate itself to the

religion and conflict

other institutions of society and to the cultural values. Yet such accommodation tends toward a coalescing of religion and power. The alliance of religion and secular power creates a situation in which apparent religiosity often conceals a deeper cynicism and a growing unbelief. Moreover, by the combination of religious and secular conservatism, a situation is produced in which social unrest and political rebellion necessarily become religious protest, and vice versa. It was only after a long period of religious wars and internal conflicts that Western man discovered that national unity and communal solidarity may be based upon values that are less than ultimate and that religious non-conformity may be permitted. Such a realization dawned only after militant efforts to establish religious conformity proved impossible. In England it was first established among Protestants. It was worked out theoretically in the philosophy of John Locke only after it had been empirically established in English history. Not until much later was the toleration extended to Catholics and Jews.

This tendency toward defensive alliance between religion and political power is related to the tendency we saw earlier for new elites to embrace a religion (or secular ideology, in our day) which gives them a sense of meaning and direction, and which legitimates their efforts and achievements. In later periods, when societies and religions are no longer in the founding and expansion stages, but on the defensive in a hostile or potentially hostile situation, the alliance of religion and power tends to be conservative and defensive.

The five dilemmas we have discussed are inherent in the process of the routinization of religious charisma. They are structural characteristics of the institutionalization process and as such are an important source of strain and conflict. They have been the cause of much protest—which, as we have seen, is a fundamental category of analysis in the study of religious movements. The conflicts of papacy and empire, and of church and state; the rise of anti-clericalism; the Reformation protest against symbolism which reached its furthest extreme in Puritanism and the left sects; the attempt of Reformation communions to return to an older form of church polity; the rejection of scholasticism, with its complex philosophical formulations, and of canon law, with its detailed legal definitions—all these indicate the importance of these dilemmas in the history of Western religion. The use of power by both Catholics and Protestants to force religious assent, and the alignments of throne and altar which followed the Great Reform in both Catholic and Protestant countries, provide examples of the fifth dilemma.

We have now seen that religion performs important functions for societies and individuals, but that these positive functions by no means exhaust the relationship of religion to social structure and to social process. Religion is involved in society in a complex way; it is intricately related to social structure and to the processes of social change. This relationship may have a positive or a negative functional significance. Often, indeed, it is ambiguous. Moreover, the strains and conflicts inherent in the relation of religion to society are increased and intensified by dilemmas inherent in the process of the institutionalization itself. We shall turn in the next chapter to a further consideration of the dysfunctional significance of religion.

97

ambiguity
and dilemma
six

We have examined religion from the point of view of both functional theory and the development of religion itself—the founding and institutionalization of specifically religious organizations. From functionalism we learned that a strategic aspect of religion, with respect to its human significance and also to its sociological function, was its concern with ultimacy and the sacred. Religion, through its relation to these, answered the problem of meaning at that point where human knowledge faltered. It provided a relationship with the beyond when human relationships no longer offered security and when human control over environing conditions failed. By its cognitive and emotional aspects religion provided an over-all sense of direction and meaning to human life, and afforded the mechanisms for an adjustment to aspects of the human situation beyond human control. From this character of religion derives its chief sociological functions, which we delineated in Chapter One.

In our consideration of the religious experience and the emergence of specifically religious organization out of it, we saw how men acted out the religious response and how this acting out and its organizational and meaningful implications became institutionalized on the three levels of ritual, belief, and organization. We saw the inner problems, the strains, the conflicts and dilemmas involved both in the development of the specifically religious organization and in the relationships which develop between the specifically religious organization and the general society. We have undertaken both an internal sociological analysis of the religious organization and an analysis of its relationship to the other institutions of society and to society as a whole.

Such a treatment has remained *functional* in an important meaning of the term. We have traced out the reciprocal relationship between religious ideas and attitudes on the one hand, and the forms of social relationships on the other. We have seen that ideas affect action, that action leads to the emergence of stable social relationships, and that social relationships "feed back" and affect ideas. For example, sectaries lead a frugal life, work hard, save and often invest, in keeping with their ideas of inner-worldly asceticism. The consequence is that they become more affluent. They consequently become more adjusted to the norms and relationships of middle class life. They become re-integrated into the middle class world of which they have become a part. As a result, the sect loses its militant opposition character and becomes routinized. It becomes a denomination, and religious beliefs are correspondingly changed in either emphasis or content.

We have seen that the ideas prevailing in a culture are interrelated in an important way with the institutions and forms of social relations prevalent in the society. In the Middle Ages, for example, the religious idea dominated, and all forms of social expression, whether conservative or revolutionary, tended to find expression in a religious idiom and in relation to religious interests. Moreover, the struggle of the medieval and renaissance middle class to improve its position in the social order became at the same time a struggle for both the approbation of new religious ideas and values, and the assertion of secular ideas and values, in opposition to the established religious ideology.

What we have seen has given us ample evidence of the fact that religion is *interconnected* with the other elements of society and culture in complex ways. Similarly, the function of religion with respect to individual personalities is a complicated one. To speak in the abstract of the function of religion or of a religious factor is apt to lead one to oversimplification. Religion seen in a concrete setting by an observer who understands its particular values and doctrines stands forth as interrelated to the other elements of society in a variety of ways. While in some cases and in some respects it is functionally positive (it performs an integrative role), to assume that to be always the case would be, in the words of a well-known sociologist of religion, Louis Schneider, "intellectually disastrous." [1]

We have seen that in other cases and in different respects the interrelationships between religion and society may indeed be, to borrow another term from Schneider, "disintegrative." What is basic in the insight of functionalism is its insistence on the "interconnectedness" of the elements of a social system and culture.[2] However, the degree of interconnectedness and its functional consequences remains in each case an empirical problem and is not to be answered from theoretical assumptions. Both Louis Schneider and

[1] Louis Schneider, "Problems in the Sociology of Religion," in *Handbook of Modern Sociology*, R. Faris (ed.) (New York: Rand McNally, 1964), p. 781.
[2] *Ibid.*, p. 777.

Robert Merton have pointed out that the "postulate of the functional unity of society," to use Merton's term, is an "empirical variable." [3]

We may summarize much of this by showing how it is possible, as a result of our examination (in the previous chapter) of the relationship of religion to conflict, to place alongside the six positive functions of religion set forth in Chapter One, six corresponding dysfunctions.

First, religion may be dysfunctional through its provision of emotional consolation and its role in bringing about reconciliation. In consoling those who are frustrated and deprived and those who have little or no stake in the social order as it exists, and by reconciling those who are alienated from society, religion may inhibit protest and act as a force impeding social changes which would prove beneficial to the welfare of society and its members. In this kind of situation religion may act as Marx indicated and become an opiate, inhibiting protest which could eventuate in a more stable society and a better adaptation of the society to its environment. By postponing reforms, this effect of religion can contribute to the build-up of explosive resentments which eventually issue in revolution and in more costly and destructive changes. In fact, the history of western Europe and the United States has shown that a vigorous conflict of interests, despite short-term dysfunctional consequences, can have long-term positive functions of a most significant kind. In Europe and America the vigorous conflict of classes and other groups led to a better distribution of the national product, a more harmonious relationship of classes, a better control of the society over its environment, and a more stable and orderly society. Religion often played a role in that history, to some extent inhibiting such conflict. It should be noted that this apparently negative function of religion actually is an aspect of its positive function of providing emotional support and consolation to its members. It represents this positive function carried too far.

Second, in the performance of the priestly function, with its relationship to a transcendent reference, religion can sacralize finite ideas and provincial attitudes to an extent which inhibits further progress in the society's knowledge of its environment and in man's efforts to control nature. The long conflict between religion and science, which has come to be symbolized by the trial of Galileo for the "crime" of suggesting that the earth revolved about the sun, offers a chief example of this kind of dysfunction. The priestly function can become embodied in a rigidly institutionalized and sacralized authoritarianism which inhibits the further development of thought in a number of directions, including religious directions. In such instances the priestly function contributes to the development not of a viable social stability but of atrophy.

Third, in sacralization of the norms and values of society, a religion can make norms of behavior, which evolved in certain specific circumstances and which lose their appropriateness under changed conditions, appear to have eternal significance. In this way it can impede a more functionally appropriate adaptation of society to changing conditions. Just as the church stubbornly refused for centuries to admit the truth of the heliocentric theory

[3] *Loc. cit.*

ambiguity and dilemma

in astronomy, so it also refused to grant the ethical legitimacy of money-lending at interest, despite the great functional need of this activity in a situation of developing capitalism. Today, in Islamic countries, religious people face religio-ethical problems concerning interest-taking similar to those faced in Medieval Europe. This sacral rigidification of norms is an element in many social conflicts and may be seen in such current issues as the discussion and conflict over birth control in the Catholic church.

Fourth, the prophetic function, so important in biblical religion, in terms of which religion provides the basis and the legitimation for criticism of and opposition to the established order, has been an important instrument for the development of a democratic society in the West. But this function can also have its dysfunctional consequences. Prophetic criticism may become so unrealistic that it beclouds genuine issues. Prophetic demands for reform may be so utopian that they constitute an obstacle in the working out of more practical action. In its concern with a transcendent rule of justice, prophetic religion may set up standards which are untimely. In its tendency to see its demands as the will of God, it may impart an extremism to the conflict that renders composition through compromise impossible. For example, while it is true that the left-wing Protestant sects of the Reformation period were the victims of intolerance—itself a consequence of religious convictions—it is also true that some of them took such extreme positions that any compromise between them and the general society was actually impossible. Thus the prophetic function can come to be an element making conflict more severe, making the evolution of realistic solutions more difficult, and exaggerating the difficulty of problems which would admit of solution in a different emotional atmosphere.

Fifth, with respect to the identity function, religion may become the object of loyalties which impede the development of new identities more appropriate to the new situations in which people find themselves. Religious identification may prove divisive to societies. Moreover, by sacralizing the identity it provides, it may worsen and in fact embitter conflict, and build deeply into the personality structures of people a recalcitrance to come to terms with an opponent. In the religious wars following the Reformation, this exacerbation of conflict by religious identifications which were central to people's self-definitions is clearly evident. Religion surrogates, such as communism and nationalism, while also providing an element of identity to people, at the same time tend to exacerbate inter-group conflicts in a way analogous to religion.

Sixth, as we have already noted in Chapter One, the relation of religion to individual maturation is an ambiguous one. Religion often plays the role of institutionalizing immaturity and develops in its adherents dependence upon religious institutions and their leaders instead of an ability to assume individual responsibility and self-direction. While this is a difficult area to assess, or even to discuss, without an appeal to one's own values, there is an obviously important empirical problem involved here. The evidence we do have suggests that religion's role with respect to individual development and maturation is highly problematic.

101

Dostoyevsky has formulated in the sharpest possible terms the dilemma of institutionalized religion, with its priestly authority, in relation to the development of individual maturity, in a profound passage which he puts into the mouth of Ivan Karamazov in the Grand Inquisitor scene in his monumental novel, *The Brothers Karamazov*. In this tale, Christ returns to this world during the time of the Inquisition in Spain. He is recognized and hailed by the people, but placed under arrest by the authorities. He is brought before the Grand Inquisitor and is silent in his presence, as he was silent long ago before Pilate. The Grand Inquisitor, in a long and impressive speech, upbraids him and points out that institutionalized religion provides happiness and security for great numbers and that Christ has no right to come back to disturb this happy condition.

What canst Thou say, indeed? I know too well what Thou wouldst say. And Thou hast no right to add anything to what Thou hadst said of old. Why, then, art Thou come to hinder us? For Thou hast come to hinder us, and Thou knowest that. But dost Thou know what will be tomorrow? I know not who Thou art and care not to know whether it is Thou or only a semblance of Him. But tomorrow I shall condemn Thee and burn Thee at the stake as the worst of heretics. And the very people who have today kissed Thy feet, tomorrow at the faintest sign from me will rush to heap up the embers of Thy fire. Knowest Thou that?

The Inquisitor explains to Christ that men are too weak to follow the exalted ideal of freedom which he proclaimed. "But Thou didst think too highly of men . . . for they are slaves, of course, though rebellious by nature." The Inquisitor states that a religion of freedom and love will not work. He says:

We have taken the sword of Caesar, and in taking it, of course, have rejected Thee and followed *him*. . . . We are told that the harlot who sits upon the beast, and holds in her hands the *mystery*, shall be put to shame, that the weak will rise up again, and will rend her royal purple and will strip naked her loathsome body. But then I will stand up and point out to Thee the thousand millions of happy creatures who have known no sin. And we who have taken their sins upon us for their happiness will stand up before Thee and say: "Judge us if Thou canst and darest." Know that I fear Thee not. Know that I too have been in the wilderness, I too have lived on roots and locusts, I too have prized the freedom with which Thou hast blessed men, and I too was striving to stand among Thy elect, among the strong and powerful, thirsting "to make up the number." But I awakened and would not serve madness. I turned back and joined the ranks of those *who have corrected Thy work*. I left the proud and went back to the humble, for the happiness of the humble.

Dostoyevsky clearly sees established religion as a form of institutionalized immaturity and dependence for the multitude, a situation he deplores. But he also indicates that perhaps such a condition is unavoidable, and indeed may even have positive significance. He poses the dilemma he sees here in the ending of Ivan Karamazov's speech:

102

When the Inquisitor stopped speaking he waited some time for his Prisoner to answer him. His silence weighed down upon him. He saw that the Prisoner had listened carefully all the time, looking gently in his face. But evidently he did not want to reply. The old man longed for Him to say something, however bitter and terrible. But He suddenly approached the old man in silence and softly kissed him on the forehead. That was his answer. The old man shuddered. His lips moved. He went to the door, opened it and said to Him: "Go, and come no more. . . . Come not at all, never, never!" And he let Him out into the dark alleys of the town. The Prisoner went away.

As for the Inquisitor, "The kiss glows in his heart, but the old man holds to his idea." [4] Thus, according to Dostoyevsky, is emotional security, and with it order and tranquility in society, purchased at the price of individual immaturity and collective bondage. While his insight is profound and deserves serious contemplation by students of religion, Dostoyevsky's treatment of this dilemma is not definitive. As we suggested earlier, the relation of religion to maturation is a complex one and a problematic one. Religion can provide the necessary elements of security and definition at certain stages of life, to enable the individual to meet crises successfully and to develop a mature personality. Paradoxically, even in its dysfunctional promotion of dependence and immaturity, it can become a focus for the development of independence and maturity by becoming the object of conflict and rejection. From this process the development of a more mature attitude and point of view, either religious or irreligious, can take place. Obviously this is a function of religion needing much more empirical research.

Religion, then, can be not simply a factor contributing to the integration of society, to the enhancement of its goals and the strengthening of its social control. It can be not simply a factor contributing to the morale and balance of individual personalities. It can also be disintegrative—a cause of strain and conflict (both individual and social), an obstacle to optimum adaptation, and a hindrance in the way of socially necessary reorganizations. Its relation to society is often a matter of ambiguity and dilemma. It will be noted that it is precisely those aspects of religion that enable it to have a positive function in society which, in changed circumstances or with the passage of time, turn into factors having the opposite significance. The relationship of religion to society is a *dialectical* one; it is one in which a factor, at one time positive and integrative in function, can become negative and disintegrative.

Religion can support the society by providing consolation to the deprived, but by the same process it can inhibit necessary changes and adjustment and cause severe functional problems. Religion provides over-all definition of the human situation, and grounds that definition in a deeper transcendent source. However, by the same token it often sacralizes ideas, which then stand as obstacles to the development of knowledge and to a better adaptation of the society to its environment. Religion supports social

---

[4] Summarized and quoted from Feodor Dostoyevsky, *The Brothers Karamazov*, Manuel Komroff (ed.) (New York: New American Library, 1957), pp. 227–242.

ambiguity and dilemma

control by sacralizing norms, but by the same process it can maintain norms no longer appropriate to changed conditions by regarding them as of sacred significance. Religion through its prophetic function can prevent an idolization of social forms which would inhibit development of an optimum of stability and adaptation, but in the same way it can, as we have seen, fan the flames of conflict and thus contribute to disorganization and chaos. Religion can provide a fundamental identity for individuals and groups, and thereby contribute to their basic morale and self-direction, but on the other hand it can by these deeds also impede the shedding of inappropriate, outdated identities, thus dividing people along religious lines and again contributing to conflict and disorganization. Finally, religion can, we know, give support to the individual in the stages of growth and maturation, but likewise it can fixate the individual in dependent and immature relationships.

This dialectical relationship is to be seen in various manifestations. What is needed, however, is much more precise and detailed knowledge of the *conditions in which* and the *mechanisms through which* this dialectical transformation of positive into ambiguous or negative functions takes place. This is an area in which much more empirical research needs to be done. Louis Schneider, whom we have quoted above, in another treatment of social change has pointed out that in sociology we need to move into the "detailed analysis of dialectically relevant mechanisms" involved in dialectical social developments. He points out that these must be understood in relation to the functional interrelatedness of social variables—to such phenomena as "feedback." [5] When a positive function, such as the provision of an overall definition of a human situation, becomes a negative one blocking further development of knowledge and better adjustment of society to changing conditions, then this result "feeds back" upon religious ideas and affects the original definition of the human situation involved. In Western history it has tended to make such ideational complexes rigid and those who hold them defensive. However, only when much more detailed empirical work has been done can a theoretically adequate statement of the conditions and mechanisms involved in such change be made.

This dialectical character of the relation of religion to society can be seen again in the ambiguity and elements of dilemma involved in the relationship of religion to democracy. It is true that the development of democratic society in the West owes much to religion, and especially to the protest elements in prophetic religion expressed historically in non-conformity. There is, nevertheless, an inherent dilemma involved in the relationship between a religion of transcendence, and democratic institutions. Religions of transcendence are conducive to the development and maintenance of democratic institutions with respect to three important characteristics of such religions. First, by providing a transcendental reference, such religions give men a higher authority, and a higher court of appeal, standing above the established institutions of society. Thus men are enabled to challenge and criticize effec-

[5] Louis Schneider, "Toward Assessment of Sorokin's View of Change," in *Explorations in Social Change*, G. Zollschan and W. Hirsch (eds.) (New York: Houghton Mifflin, 1964), pp. 371–400, p. 385.

ambiguity and dilemma

tively the contemporary workings of society and the policies of its elites. Secondly, the same prophetic element, by relating men to God, contributes to the autonomy and dignity of the individual by making the individual person more than a mere member of the group or the society. Not only are protest and criticism legitimated, but individual welfare and dignity are not simply subordinated to group demands. The individual is thus enabled to stand to some degree outside institutionalized forms, to criticize them and hence to change them. Also, the emphasis of such religions upon personal ethical responsibility, related often to an ethic of self-control, contributes to the development of ethically responsible citizens, a requisite for the successful functioning of democratic systems. Third, the doctrine of universalism and brotherhood preached by such religions represents one important source of democratic ideals and reinforces them in life. In these ways, religions of transcendence perform important positive functions in a democratic society.

However, the dilemma involved here is genuine. The very elements which contribute positively to the functioning of democracy can come into serious conflict with it. With the institutionalization of religion, the transcendental reference from which it derives its ascendency over other institutional patterns tends to become identified with the ecclesiastical power structure, and hence a clerical authoritarianism can develop. The church then becomes the earthly embodiment of what are regarded as transcendent elements, and genuine transcendence over institutionalized forms, including the institutionalized forms of religion, tends to be lost. And, too, the church as a sacred entity tends to inhibit criticism of itself and of the social order with which it has become accommodated. Thus the original source of the prophetic element—the transcendental reference—which made possible criticism and protest, is transformed into a sacralization of established forms and becomes an inhibiting mechanism with respect to both protest and criticism.

The ethic of personal responsibility, so crucial to the functioning of democracy, can also develop in the direction of inflexibility and come to exhibit a narrow and doctrinaire rigidity. The result is a spirit of intolerance which proves to be dysfunctional for democratic institutions, which require flexible give-and-take in dialogue and discussion if they are to function at all. This is particularly the case in pluralistic societies composed of people with both diverse religious faiths and no religious faith, in which widely divergent points of view must be accommodated in an on-going consensus of courses of action. It must be further noted that since institutionalization tends towards a crystallization of established forms, and since the secularization of culture often makes for defensiveness on the part of religious people, tendencies toward authoritarianism and rigidity are increased. Finally, the ethic of brotherhood can come to conflict with the ideal of universality, and there can develop a sacralized in-group allegiance which becomes divisive to democratic society and injurious to the common weal. Again, defensiveness against the threat of secularization, by way of eliciting solidarity from the members of a religious group in the face of an alien danger, can increase this tendency considerably.

The inherent tension between the church and the world, which was analyzed by Troeltsch and which we considered in Chapter Four, has a positive functional significance for democratic societies and for religious organizations themselves. Democratic societies require certain values, among which the worth of the individual, an ethic of social justice, and the priority of the general welfare over individual and sub-group interests are strategic. These values in the West owe much to prophetic and evangelical religion—to the prophets and the gospel—and to secularized social movements whose values have been remotely derived from such religious sources. But, as we have seen, religions of transcendence can maintain this basis for criticism and dissent—can maintain ideas of individual worth, social justice, and the general welfare—against dominant vested interests of ruling and influential elites, only if such religions do not become so well accommodated to society that the genuine sense of transcendence is lost. In cases of accommodation where it is lost, the inherent tension and strain between the church and the world and between ideal and practical values is compromised out of existence. Consequently, a basic function of religion in democratic society is lost. However, unless some degree of compromise and accommodation takes place, the warfare of church and state, and the conflict between religion and other spheres of human endeavor, can prove disruptive to the society.

However, if religion compromises with the general society to such an extent that church loyalty in the sense of allegiance to ecclesiastical authorities becomes synonymous with religion, the prophetic and gospel elements of transcendence are lost. Religion becomes but one more institution adjusted to the prevailing winds of dominant opinion. In such cases the basic function of a religion of transcendence in democratic society is lost and the religion of transcendence is itself transformed into an acceptance of provincial and less-than-ultimate ideals. If religions of transcendence are to remain genuinely so, and if they are to continue to contribute positively to democratic society, then a degree of "healthy unadjustment" between religion and society must remain, despite the fact that this unadjustment itself will be the source of some conflict and will have some dysfunctional consequences. We have seen in the above discussion that a conflict of interests in a society can exhibit both short-run dysfunctional consequences and long-term effects of great positive functional significance. This is particularly to be seen in the effect of the labor movement in bringing about social reform in western Europe and America, and in other liberal reform movements as well. It would appear that a similar observation may be made with respect to religion. The strain between religion and society may give rise in the short run to conflicts which prove disruptive to some degree of stability and harmony within the social system, but it may prove in the long run to have important functional consequences of a positive character in preserving the very values which are requisite to a democratic society.

Religion and Magic: Functional Dilemmas

Further strains, conflicts, and functional dilemmas may be seen both in the relation of religion to magic (so often found

106

ambiguity and dilemma

empirically associated with each other) and in the relation of magic to society. In the first chapter we considered how magic contributes to human morale by allowing men to act in situations wherein they cannot alter frustrating conditions, and by giving them hope of aid through the agency of supernatural powers. This positive function of magic, emphasized by Malinowski, does not exhaust its relationship to social structures and social processes.[6] Magic also comprises a set of human activities in which men act out aggressions, find outlets for forbidden impulses, and seek to inflict injury upon their fellows. Both religion and magic enable men to adjust to disappointment, deprivation, frustration, illness, and death. They aid men to handle the problem of evil. But many kinds of magic (often called *black* magic in contrast to the socially and psychologically beneficent *white* magic, described and analyzed by Malinowski) represent an attempt by men to utilize and exploit evil for their own purposes.

In witchcraft and sorcery, people attempt to use sacred forces (often what Durkheim called "impure sacred forces") and agencies to achieve antisocial ends, and ends detrimental to the welfare of individuals. In this phenomenon we see an instructive combination of functional and dysfunctional characteristics. Witchcraft and sorcery enable men to act out aggressions which result from hostility that has been built up in them by frustrations and deprivations involved in their social conditions. It often provides a "safe" outlet for emotions which, if acted upon directly, would disrupt society. Also, the attribution of misfortune to the action of witches provides an emotionally satisfying explanation, and enables some symbolic action to be taken. Moreover, witchcraft and sorcery enable people to act out socially forbidden actions and to receive some vicarious enjoyment of forbidden urges in identification with others believed to be witches and sorcerers. To these positive psychological functions of witchcraft and sorcery must be added their social functions. Beatrice Blyth Whiting, in a study of the Paiute Indians, has shown how sorcery, by inculcating the members of the tribe with a fear of magical retaliation for evil, restrains actions which would violate the rights of others.[7] Another anthropologist who has specialized in the study of these phenomena, Deward Walker, has pointed out that this function of witchcraft and sorcery has been widely corroborated in the anthropological literature. He attests to the significance of this social control function. It is, he states, "particularly effective," since a person feels that he "must guard against not only obvious violations of individual rights, but must exert every effort to retain the good will of acquaintances."[8] Moreover, witchcraft and sorcery, by representing all that is forbidden in dramatic form —by dramatizing evil—help to set out in bold relief what is held to be moral

---

[6] See discussion in Chapter One, pp. 7–10.

[7] Beatrice B. Whiting, *Paiute Sorcery* (New York: Viking Fund Publications in Anthropology, No. 15, 1950).

[8] This discussion of witchcraft and sorcery owes much to an unpublished paper by Deward E. Walker, Jr. and a series of discussions in which he shared with me his insights to be presented in a forthcoming study of this subject.

and good. Further, religious ceremonies and benign magical rites which religious and magical specialists perform in order to counteract, undo, and ward off the evil caused by witchcraft and sorcery, reinforce and re-confirm all that is the opposite of the evil practices. Thus, by reinforcing norms, evil magic paradoxically performs a positive function for social control. The psychological functions of permitting expression and catharsis have also the sociological significance of draining off to some extent potentially disruptive emotions.

Indeed even quite obviously disruptive consequences of sorcery and witchcraft may have positive functional significance, another example of functional ambiguity. In societies and cultures in which evil magical practices are common, or at least believed by the people to be common, fear and suspicion become widespread and poison the social atmosphere between individuals and groups. In that respect magic becomes a disintegrative and negative functional element. A number of anthropologists have found, however, that in many aboriginal African societies such fears and animosities perform a positive function as well. In societies with expanding populations and limited resources in land, it becomes necessary to sub-divide the kinship group, which is the chief social unit. This segmentation of the lineage is functionally necessary and relieves the pressure of population upon limited sustenance potential. It has been found that accusations of sorcery often increase as economic pressure develops. This brings about a situation in which segmentation—a functionally positive disruption of an existing group—occurs.[9] Other anthropologists have found that accusations of sorcery and witchcraft play a positive functional role as a means of limiting the use of power by individual leaders and small groups. Such accusations provide a kind of check-and-balance mechanism, preventing a narrow concentration of power.[10]

Yet these positive functions have obviously their negative and dysfunctional aspects. Although catharsis is afforded and some action is made possible in frustrating circumstances by the use of evil magic, the forms of acting out of emotions and impulses provided by evil magic can be highly disruptive and injurious to individuals and groups. With respect to evil magic, Ruth Benedict has pointed out that: "Far from being an asset it has often been a heavy liability, and its phenomena are analogous to the delusions of grandeur and fear constructs of the neurotic." [11] Widespread fear and suspicion, efforts to ward off deeply felt but unreal threats, and attempts to inflict evil through imaginary means seem a high price to pay for the availability of avenues of catharsis and for the reinforcement of social control. It has also been observed by anthropologists that as a mechanism

---

[9] M. Marwick, "Some Problems in the Sociology of Sorcery and Witchcraft," in *African Systems of Thought*, M. Fortes and G. Dieterlen (eds.) (London: Oxford University Press, 1965), and also "Another Modern Anti-Witchcraft Movement in East Central Africa," in *Africa*, No. 2, 20:100–112.

[10] Clyde Kluckhohn, *Navaho Witchcraft* (Cambridge: Peabody Museum of Archaeology and Ethnology, 1944).

[11] Ruth Benedict, "Magic," *Encyclopedia of the Social Sciences* (1937), IX and X, p. 44.

ambiguity and dilemma

for catharsis, magic may prove quite inadequate. Such catharsis is rendered superficial by routinization and by the fact that the magical rite is often "swamped in a meticulous observance of petty rules." [12]

We have noted in Chapter Three that ideas and rites come into existence in certain situations and that they are often expressive of emotions engendered in those situations of origin. Thus, like a religious rite, a magical rite becomes a re-presentation of an original experience; it becomes a stylized and symbolic acting out of the archetypal original performance and its associated attitudes. Once the rite has been institutionalized, however, or when the idea becomes a part of established belief systems, it comes to possess an autonomy of its own. Then it "feeds back" upon the subjective dispositions of those involved and forms them after its own model.

Witchcraft and sorcery involve established rites—institutionalized within the groups which practice them—whose purpose it is to bring harm to others. Such rites obviously afford some opportunity for the acting out in symbolic form, and consequently the catharsis, of aggressive and hostile desires. But they also perform the socialization function—"the teaching and forming function"—of all established culture patterns. They elicit and help create such desires and wishes. The extent to which they offer a safety valve by draining off dangerous aggressions in symbolic directions, and the degree to which they socialize people in and thereby propagate anti-social and harmful attitudes and actions, is an empirical question to be investigated in every instance and for which no general answer is possible.

Such expressions of evil magic and such attempts to manipulate evil for human purposes are institutionalized in witchcraft and sorcery. As such they are in a condition of functional interconnectedness with the other elements of societies and cultures. Whether this interconnectedness contributes to the continued existence of society and whether it contributes positively to the functioning of human personality represents a complex empirical problem. It may be found to have a many-sided and in important respects ambiguous function, as what we have said above indicates.

It is a considerable contribution of functionalists both in sociology and anthropology to point out that evil magic can indeed have positive functional consequences for a society, and for the expressive needs of individuals under conditions of frustration. Indeed, unless it had some such functions, it is difficult to see why it would exist at all. Without meeting some human needs and without some integration into the going society, witchcraft and sorcery would not survive in a society. But the question remains as to whether or not it may have more deleterious than positive effects. An analogy with biology is suggestive here. Many fevers which rack the body represent the mobilization of the organism to fight off an invasion by foreign organisms—yet, extremes of fever may be a cause of death. There is obviously a limit to the positive significance of such functionalism.

It would appear that the witchcraft fanaticism of the early period of modern Western history had the functional significance of permitting

[12] *Ibid.*, p. 43.

expression of pent-up emotions of hostility both in magical activity, and in hunting down, prosecuting, and punishing those believed to be engaged in it. These feelings of fear and hostility, arising from a number of sources internal and external to late medieval and early modern Europe, and displaced upon witchcraft, found expression in witch hunts and inquisitorial practices. They thereby became intimately associated with both religion and politics. Belief in witchcraft, and its legal prosecution, became important elements in the public life of the age. One may well question whether its role in providing catharsis for feelings of hostility and fear, and in reinforcing the ethical norms which witchcraft defied (reinforcing through public participation in the activities of hunting down those believed to be witches, and in public attendance at executions) was the best functional complex of mechanisms to handle the problems involved. Did not the medicine prove more deadly than the disease?

There is much compelling evidence to suggest that the fears and hostility of the period were made worse by witchcraft and sorcery, and that the specific problems facing the society were rendered more difficult to solve. It was a time when religious uniformity, until then the basis of political units, was being challenged by the more varied and many-sided culture which had developed in the European cities from the twelfth century. The witchcraft craze no doubt reflected the fears and anxieties caused by this upsetting experience. But it is also true that belief in the reality of witchcraft and sorcery and the institutionalization of juridical methods of handling what was believed to be diabolical magic resulted in the superimposition of additional fears and animosities onto the religious problems and religious divisions of the age. It was also a time of severe power conflicts, which were complicated and exacerbated by the involvement of competing religious ideologies in political rivalries. A conflict between England and Spain over colonial spoils, for example, was made more severe by the fact that England was the defender of the Protestant faith, while the Spanish monarchy was staunchly and militantly Catholic. The witchcraft phenomena also became a part of power conflicts in these European societies. In this situation genuine acts of secret aggression, such as in poisonings, and suspicion of and attempts at recourse to black magic introduced additional fear and hostility into already conflict-laden conditions. It has been said of European witchcraft in those days that "all classes were affected and concerned from Pope to peasant, from Queen to cottage girl."

Witchcraft itself as a believed and accepted practice obviously became some form of organized behavior contravening the established norms and values. The general suspicion of it and the prosecution of it by the authorities became a mode of reasserting the norms and values of the society. But it also became a permissible mode of expression of strong anti-social impulses and dangerous hostilities. The elements of fanaticism, violence, and unreality involved call into question the functional efficacy of such outbreaks of "social fevers." It appears that by such methods of catharsis and social control, dangerous and disruptive animosities are propagated and more harm

110

is done to the social order than can possibly be compensated for by their minimal positive functional significance.

In the late medieval and early modern periods of European history, witchcraft was believed in by "the profoundest thinkers, the acutest minds" of the time.[13] One of the most important and illustrious legal minds of the sixteenth century, Jean Bodin (1530–1590) believed "that there existed, not only in France, a complete organization of witches, immensely wealthy, of almost infinite potentialities, most cleverly captained, with centers and cells in every district, utilizing an espionage in every land, with high placed adherents at court, with humble servitors in the cottage. This organization, witchcraft, maintained a relentless and ruthless war against the prevailing order and settled state. No design was too treacherous, no betrayal was too cowardly, no blackmail too base and foul." [14] Witchcraft and its prosecution obviously encouraged, elicited, and helped to create as well as to displace from other objects, fears and hostilities which had marked destructive consequences in fanatical conflicts in both legal and extra-legal form.

The functional significance of such a phenomenon is obviously analogous to that of a fever in the physical organism. It performs some psychological and social functions, or else it would not continue to exist, but it exacts a heavy dysfunctional price in doing so. It may be said to be functional, to use another analogy, as a neurosis is functional to the individual personality. In fact such forms of collective behavior display interesting and significant resemblances to forms of neurosis and even psychosis. A neurosis is a distorted way of handling one's emotions and one's situation; it is a mode of adaptation involving unreal elements, seen as part of reality, and the expression of inappropriate emotions. But it has the functional significance for the individual of providing some mode of handling difficult emotions and situations. The individual is enabled to respond somehow. But such neurotic modes of adaptation prove inadequate. They stand in the way of developing more realistic and more favorable methods and responses to one's world. The same can be said with respect to evil magic. While witchcraft and sorcery provide outlets for dangerous emotions, and while they become integrated to some extent into the social control mechanism of the culture, they also encourage socially disruptive tendencies, distort reality and infuse definitions of reality with unreal fantasy elements, and give rise to widespread fear, suspicion, and animosity. At best, evil magical practices offer "mechanisms of displacement." Displacing emotions may have the positive effect of channeling off dangerous acts into fantasy areas, and thereby preventing real damaging action from taking place. It may also have the effect of distracting

---

[13] Heinrich Kramer and James Sprenger, *Malleus Maleficarum*, trans. by Montague Summers (London: Pushkin Press, 1951), p. xiii. This work (the title means *The Witch Hammer*) appeared in its first Latin edition most likely in 1486. There were 14 editions between 1487 and 1520, and some 16 or so between 1574 and 1669. It played a very important role in hunting down and prosecuting witches in both Catholic and Protestant countries.

[14] *Loc. cit.*

attention from problems that could be solved if given realistic attention. Indeed, such displacement tends "in both primitive and modern societies to substitute unreal achievement for real." [15]

In Chapter Two, we saw that it was insufficient in studying religion to ask simply the functional questions: What does religion do to and for society? What to and for the individual? We found it necessary to understand the content, the meaning, of religious beliefs and practices. We had to consider the content of the religious experience and to ask what kind of meanings and what kind of attitudes are being acted out in the ritual re-enactment of it in religious liturgies. Only on this basis could one comprehend the significance of cult, belief, and religious organization, and their complex interrelations with other aspects of society and culture. Similarly, we must ask the questions: What is the content—the meaning and related attitudes toward others—involved in magical attempts to exploit and manipulate evil forces? What impulses and wishes are being acted out? What is their implication for social relations? Moreover, like the religious ritual which not only re-enacts but elicits and helps to form attitudes and emotions, the magical ritual elicits and helps to form attitudes and emotions as well. Thus it propagates and helps to create anti-social attitudes and acts.

To ask the question of content is to open up an area of great significance for the social sciences. The deeper impulses which find expression in black magic need to be understood better than they are, as do the social and psychological conditions which engender them. That such practices relate to deeper problems of personality psychology is also clear. The great authoritative book, written in the late fifteenth century, which was used as the handbook for detecting and combatting witchcraft in the West, the *Malleus Malificarum*, states that "All witchcraft comes from carnal lust." [16] Its content suggests that repressed sexuality and aggression were important psychological elements involved in evil magic. The book tells of the varied consequences of such magic, including such diversities as the causing of hailstorms, injury to cattle, and murder. Obviously this is an area in which more research is nescessary and in which disciplines such as anthropology and sociology should cooperate with psychiatry and clinical psychology.

Religion as a Central Element in Culture

The question of whether religion and magic perform a positive, a negative, or an ambiguous role in society is not simply the question of the nature of their contribution to social stability and to maintenance of the existing social system. Societies are themselves often dynamic entities, subject to long- and short-term processes of change caused by both internal and external factors. New technological developments, such as seen in the Industrial Revolution in Europe and America or in the developmental efforts in the new nations of today; internal developments in religion, such as the

[15] Benedict, *op. cit.*, p. 44.
[16] Kramer and Sprenger, *op. cit.*, p. 47.

112

ambiguity and dilemma

Reformation, or in government, such as serious reform or revolution; problems involving defense and war—all these contribute to the initiation and continuation of social change. We have seen that religion may be related to the changes involved in a variety of ways. It may be an initiator and promoter of change, or its stubborn and recalcitrant opponent. It may be centrally involved in change, or peripheral to the areas of decisive change in a society, and only much later experience its effects.

Religious organizations may be variously related to the new organizations which change brings into existence. Thus at times in Western history, the church found itself in conflict with the development of the state, and later with the development of the nation-state. At other times and in other places, however, the church was an important support for such political developments. Religious beliefs—ideas and values—may also be variously related to such change. New discoveries in science have in the past been in conflict with established religious ideas. On the other hand, established religious ideas have been important in creating attitudes favorable to scientific endeavor. New ideas or new discoveries concerning the biological or social make-up of man may conflict with religious and ethical beliefs. The relation of religion to social development and change can indeed be positive, negative, or complicatedly ambiguous. In every case the problems in this area remain empirical ones, to be tested in research and not to be solved by deduction from theoretical postulates.

Religion is a central and fundamentally important aspect of culture and, like culture as a whole, its concrete content may be in harmony or in conflict with situations existing in, or transformations in progress in, the society. A consideration of religion as a core element in culture will help us to summarize the human significance of religion. Like culture, religion may be described as a "Dramatic Design," serving "to redeem the sense of flux by investing passage and process with the appearance of aim, purpose, and historical form." [17] Religion, like culture, is a symbolic transformation of experience. The design which religion lends to life is regarded by the religious person as a revelation, natural or supernatural, of the deeper meaning of experience. It is seen by the sceptic as a set of conventions concealing chance events and a vast cosmic indifference to human concerns. It has been said that "culture in the sense of form is man's supreme, albeit most ambiguous, discovery. Were it not for the intervention of human concern, the flux of nature and time would seem without distinction and direction." [18]

Like culture, religion is in one important respect a "Defensive System" —that is, it is comprised of "an array of beliefs and attitudes which help to defend us against vexing doubts, anxieties and aggressions." Religion is one of "culture's protective forms" through which, consciously and unconsciously, the fears and aggressions "generated within individuals and societies are per-

[17] Benjamin Nelson, "Self Images and Systems of Spiritual Direction in the History of European Civilization," in The Quest for Self-Control: Classical Philosophies and Scientific Research, Samuel Z. Klausner (ed.) (New York: Free Press of Glencoe, 1965), p. 53.

[18] Ibid., p. 53.

ceived to be mitigated." [19] Thirdly, like culture, religion is also a "Directive System." It is made up of normative elements which shape and form our responses on many levels of thinking, feeling, and acting. It makes us "perceive, feel, think and perform in desired ways." [20] Finally, like culture, religion involves a "Symbol Economy." It involves the allocation of symbolic values of varied worth.[21]

Religion, seen as central to culture and representing the ultimate and sacred aspects of culture, represents a mode of human consciousness involving its own symbolic forms. Like all complexes of ideas and all perspectives upon the world—like all systems of symbols—held by men, it is interconnected with other patterns of thought and with complexes of human relationships in societies—with institutions—in a variety of ways. However, the ultimate and sacral character of religion introduces a distinctive element into religion. As a result of this ultimate and sacral character, religion presents a dilemma in terms of its functional significance. It is a three-sided dilemma to which we must now turn.

Religion and Society:
A Fundamental Dilemma

The relationship of religion and society presents to the sociologists a fundamental dilemma, of which three aspects may be distinguished. First of all, religion concerns man at the limit-situation, at that point at which awareness of ultimacy arises. Here the problems of ultimate meaning and of man's place in the over-all scheme of things come to the fore. They arise with an urgency best characterized by the modern word "existential." Secondly, religion is concerned with the sacred—that is, it involves a specific mode of apprehension and response which calls for intense awe and profound respect for its object. It is a mode of consciousness that is radically other, fundamentally heterogeneous, with respect to the secular or profane sphere of human concern and action. Thirdly, religion is based upon faith— that is, its object is supraempirical and its tenets do not admit of empirical demonstration or proof.

A sharp contrast is revealed if religion in these respects be compared to the institutions in whose context economic activities are carried on. In economic action—production and exchange of commodities—less-than-ultimate values are involved and less-than-total relationships with persons are developed. Moreover, the values involved are mainly consummatory or instrumental in character—they are concerned with things to be consumed or or used. Hence such activities are secular or profane rather than sacred. Finally, the values and procedures of economic life appear to be based upon more obvious empirical assumptions, assumptions more readily tested in mundane experience, more readily experienced and more easily confirmed in the empirical here-and-now. In other fields of human endeavor, such as law and education, we may observe a condition in which the two spheres, so

[19] *Ibid.*, pp. 53 and 54.   [20] *Ibid.*, p. 53.   [21] *Ibid.*, p. 53.

ambiguity and dilemma

sharply segregated in the comparison of religion and economic life, are found somewhat mixed. In a courtroom there is a definite sacral element, as there is in the procedures of legal action. In learning, the concern with truth points toward ultimacy, and indeed often exhibits a covertly sacred character.

The examination of the religious experience shows us that men respond to a "beyond," to the "ultimate" as "sacred." It also points to man's need for an ultimate answer to the problem of life's meaning, and for an ultimate relationship to some kind of "ground" of being. This "ground" is seen as undergirding the world of experience, though not itself directly experienced. From these three elements—ultimacy, sacredness, and reliance upon faith— derives the three-sided fundamental dilemma of religion in human life. It is clear that most of life must be lived in the sphere of the profane, the everyday—in the realm of the less-than-ultimate concerns, activities, and relationships. How is the demand of ultimacy to be related to the requirements of mundane existence? How is the response to and relationship to the sacred to be put together with the radically other practical demands of the profane sphere? Durkheim, in *The Elementary Forms of the Religious Life*, describes one solution: the patterned alternation of sacred and profane periods, of periods of celebration and periods of work. Religiously dominated societies, such as that of medieval Christendom, have utilized this method and have alternated work periods with periods given over to sacred or recreational activities; often to the both combined. Sombart, whose early sociological studies of economic life are still of great interest, has shown that in the Bavarian mining industry in the sixteenth century, "in one case, out of a total of 203 days, only 123 were working days; in another, out of 161 days 99 were working days; in a third, out of 287 days 193 were working days." [22] Moreover, in societies which have not been secularized to any considerable degree, worldly activities such as work, government, learning, etc., are surrounded by religious observances—prayers, reading of sacred scriptures, singing of hymns, etc., at the beginning and end of work periods. But the pragmatic demands of less-than-ultimate daily existence, with its down-to-earth requirements, its less-than-ultimate values, its routinized procedures, and its emphasis upon use and consumption, act as a secularizing agent. The sense of both the ultimate and the sacred tend to be lost. The dilemma of relating these incompatible elements is characteristic of all societies, but with the secularization of culture, it becomes more palpable and more profound.

Finally, there is the dilemma presented by the intimate but incompatible relationship that exists between faith and doubt. Religion is based upon faith; faith, by the very fact that it involves an assent to tenets which transcend experience, involves the possibility of doubt. Were there no doubt there could be no faith, there would simply be knowledge. We have seen that what is experienced at the limit-situation in the religious experience remains supraempirical; it is not directly experienced by the senses in a manner analogous to mundane experience, and it is beyond adequate conceptual formulation. Since religious organizations embody and seek to prolong and

---

[22] Werner Sombart, *The Quintessence of Capitalism*, trans. and ed. by M. Epstein New York: E. P. Dutton, 1915), p. 19.

re-enact the religious experience, they come to embody the inherent dilemm. implied in the religious experience as well. Religious institutions or organiza tions must in some fashion show forth the sacred and the ultimate, althoug as human institutions and organizations they are less-than-ultimate and in deed often are quite secular in procedures and performance. They rest upo certain beliefs which their members hold, which are matters of faith rathe than of knowledge. Since faith is intimately related to doubt, the religiou institution and organization possesses an inherent element of instability, o potential instability; it is built into its very framework.

In everyday life, faith is largely supported by social convention. Con sensus lends an air of spurious self-evidentness to ideas and beliefs held i common, though such ideas and beliefs actually be of a supraempirical chai acter. Yet human beings are always capable of going in their consciousnes to the limit-situation; they are potentially capable of transcending the estab lished modes of thought. When circumstances are propitious, men may as new questions, pose new problems. Consequently, men have the capacity t break through prescribed and consensually validated doctrines and practice doubting their truth and questioning their adequacy and efficacy. Moreove since religion provides an important means for the acting out of expressiv needs, forms of ritual which evolved in an earlier period may prove inade quate for the expression and acting out of expressive needs in new situation When this happens men search for new forms, and often evolve them i rebellion against those already existing. Such revolt against established form of worship constituted a major element in the Protestant Reformation. Grad ual changes in the conditions of life in a society affect the psychologica make-up of individuals and can render older symbolic forms irrelevant. S cial change and increased knowledge—in fact, any kind of new experience— may alter men's perspective upon the world, their society, and themselve and as a consequence they may find established ideas unconvincing. All o these developments tend to bring men to the limit-situation. All of then tend to create situations which engender doubt.

Religion as a central element in culture provides form and direction t human thought, feeling, and action. It stabilizes human orientations, value aspirations and ego-ideals. But religion rests upon faith—upon an assent t the supraempirical. Consequently, all those other elements of values, aspira tions, and goals which its undergirds, rest, like religion itself, upon an unstab base. In secularized societies, the instability of religion, and of other value derived from it, becomes apparent to a degree that would have been though impossible in older, traditional societies.

Thus religion reveals itself as exhibiting this fundamental three-side dilemma, not accidental or tributary, but essential and central to its ver structure. Religious men must live in relationship with two incompatible an heterogeneous realms of experience; they must maintain relations with bot the sacred and the profane; and they must live concerned with both the ult mate and the mundane. From this situation there derives a host of prol lems for religious institutions. One example may be seen in the attempt c Christians to maintain the spirit of the New Testament and the primitiv church in the changed conditions of the later centuries. The result was tha

116

monasticism, with its ascetic way of life, came to be the Christian ideal for both religious and layman alike. This monastic conception failed to do justice to the importance of upper and middle class activities and caused lay revolt against Christianity itself. Moreover, the conflict between the sacred and profane spheres—their radical heterogeneity—lies at the basis of a number of important religious conflicts, especially those we have examined between the church and world. This heterogeneity of the sacred and the profane renders religious charisma especially unstable and makes the institutionlization of religion particularly necessary to the survival of religion itself. But, as we have seen, institutionalization involves routinization, and consequently charisma is diminished and everydayness is introduced. From these conditions are derived the five dilemmas of the institutionalization of religion presented in Chapter Five. The specific form and content of these dilemmas will vary in different cultural settings. They are, however, built-in sources of strain and are called dilemmas precisely because they are not merely problms. Problems admit of solution; dilemmas are inescapable paradoxes which must be lived with and handled in some way, but which cannot be eliminated. Indeed, our whole study has indicated that the relationship between religion and society is in fact a great dilemma which works itself out in the concrete sources of strain and conflict and in the more specific dilemmas we have considered.

The sociology of religion is the study of the significant, and often subtle, relationships which prevail between religion and social structure, and between religion and social processes. It involves the attempt to develop and make more adequate its own conceptualizations as it comes to comprehend better the many-sided phenomena which religion presents for study. It offers modern man an important avenue for the better understanding of religion as a human concern and human activity. As such, it makes a contribution to the development of man's understanding of himself, his behavior, his thought and feeling, and his relationships to his fellow man as embodied in his society. As one application of sociology to a specific field of human interest, and as an academic discipline, it is young—but it offers the possibility of a promising future. Since religion is related to deeper human needs, feelings, and aspirations; since it deals with some of the most profound aspects of the human condition; and since its meaning and function in both these respects are still quite mysterious to us, the prospects of further study and research in this field issue an attractive and exciting challenge to those interested in furthering the study of man.

The sociology of religion does not concern itself with the truth or worth of the supraempirical beliefs upon which religion rests. It is concerned with the effects of these in the historical experience of men and in the development of human societies. Although it takes a naturalistic approach as a methodological rule, it does not pass judgment upon questions of faith itself. Yet it does provide empirical information and ways of looking at religious phenomena without which an intelligent and sophisticated approach to religion is no longer possible in our day. For itself, it says with Alexander Pope:

Presume not God to scan
The proper study of mankind is man.

117

selected references

This is a set of selected readings, not a comprehensive bibliography.

Concerning functional theory, see Kingsley Davis, *Human Society*, (New York: Macmillan, 1948); Robert K. Merton, "Manifest and Latent Functions," in *Social Theory and Social Structure*, (Glencoe, Ill., The Free Press, 1957) pp. 19–84; Emile Durkheim, *The Elementary Forms of the Religious Life*, trans. by Joseph Ward Swain, (Glencoe, Ill.: The Free Press, 1954); J. Milton Yinger, *Religion, Society and the Individual*, (New York: Macmillan, 1957); William J. Goode, *Religion Among the Primitives*, (Glencoe, Ill.: The Free Press, 1951); Talcott Parsons, "The Sociology of Religion," in *Essays in Sociological Theory*, (Glencoe, Ill.: The Free Press, 1958) and Louis Schneider, "Problems in the Sociology of Religion," in *Handbook of Modern Sociology*, R. Faris (ed.) (New York: Rand McNally, 1964). For anthropological works see Clyde Kluckhohn, *Navaho Witchcraft*, Peabody Museum Papers, No. XXIII, (Cambridge, Mass.: Harvard University Press, 1944); Bronislaw Malinowski, *Magic, Science and Religion*, (Garden City, N. Y.: Doubleday Anchor Books, 1954); and Robert Lowie, *Primitive Religion*, (New York: Boni and Liveright, 1924).

With respect to the religious experience, in addition to the Durkheim listed above, see Rudolf Otto, *The Idea of the Holy*, trans. by J. W. Harvey, (London: Oxford University Press, 1950); G. Van der Leeuw, *Religion In Essence and Manifestation*, Vols. I and II (New York: Harper Torchbooks, 1963) and Mircea Eliade, *Patterns in Comparative Religion*, trans. by Rosemary Sheed (New York: Sheed and Ward, 1958). Concerning charisma, see Max Weber, *The Theory of Social and Economic Organization*, trans. by A. M. Henderson and Talcott Parsons, (New York: Oxford University Press, 1947), pp. 358–388.

On the institutionalization of religion and the strains, conflicts and dilemmas involved in the relation of religious organizations and the general society, see Ernst Troeltsch, *The Social Teachings of the Christian Churches*, trans. by Olive Wyon, (New York: Macmillan, 1931); Joachim Wach, *Sociology of Religion*,

(Chicago: University of Chicago Press, 1944); H. Richard Neibuhr, *The Social Sources of Denominationalism*, (New York: Henry Holt, 1929); Arthur E Bestor, Jr., *Backwoods Utopias: The Sectarian and Owenite Phases of Communitarian Socialism in America: 1663–1829* (Philadelphia: University of Pennsylvania Press, 1950); Bryan R. Wilson, *Sects and Society*, (Berkeley: University of California Press, 1961); Thomas F. O'Dea *The Mormons*, (Chicago: University of Chicago Press, 1957); Max Weber, *The Protestant Ethic and the Spirit of Capitalism*, trans. by Talcott Parsons, (New York: Scribners, 1930); *The Religion of China*, trans. by Hans H. Gerth (Glencoe Ill.: The Free Press, 1951); *Ancient Judaism*, trans. by Hans H. Gerth and Don Martindale (Glencoe, Ill.: The Free Press, 1952); *The Religion of India*, trans. by Hans H. Gerth and Don Martindale (Glencoe, Ill.: The Free Press, 1958) and in *From Max Weber: Essays in Sociology* trans. and ed. by Hans H. Gerth and C Wright Mills, (New York: Oxford University Press, 1946); "The Social Psychology of the World Religions," pp. 267–301 "The Protestant Sects and the Spirit of Capitalism," pp. 302–322; and "Religious Rejections of the World and Their Directions," pp. 323–359. Also see R. H. Tawney, *Religion and the Rise of Capitalism* (New York: Penguin Books, 1947) Amintore Fanfani, *Catholicism, Protestantism and Capitalism*, (London: Sheed and Ward, 1935); Sidney A. Burrell, (ed.) *The Role of Religion in Modern European History*, (New York: Macmillan, 1964) Karl Marx and Friedrich Engels, *On Religion*, (New York: Schocken Books 1964) and Karl Mannheim, *Ideology and Utopia*, (New York: Harcourt, Brace & World, 1936).

Also of general interest are the following titles: Gerhard Lenski, *The Religious Factor: A Sociological Study of Religion's Impact on Politics, Economics and Family Life*, (Garden City, New York: Doubleday, 1961); Kenneth W. Underwood *Protestant and Catholic*, (Boston: Beacon Press, 1957); John J. Kane, *Catholic Protestant Conflicts in America* (Chicago Regnery, 1955); Will Herberg, *Protestant Catholic, Jew* (Garden City, N. Y Doubleday, 1955); Marshall Sklare, *Conservative Judaism*, (Glencoe, Ill.; Th Free Press, 1955); Robert N. Bellah *Tokagawa Religion*, Glencoe, Ill.: The Free Press, 1958); Vittorio Lanternari, *The Religions of the Oppressed*, trans. by Lisa Sergio, (New York: New American Library, 1965); Thomas F. O'Dea, *America Catholic Dilemma*, (New York: Sheed and Ward, 1958); Sister Marie Augusta Neal S.N.D., *Values and Interest in Social Change* (Englewood Cliffs, N. J.: Prentice-Hall, 1965).

118

index

120